Mount Moran from Leigh Lake

A Sierra Club Totebook®

Hiking
the
Teton
Backcountry

by Paul Lawrence

Sierra Club Books • San Francisco

Copyright © 1973 by the Sierra Club.
Photographs by the author.
All rights reserved.
Library of Congress Catalog Card Number 73-79896.
International Standard Book Number 87156-092-5.
Manufactured in the United States of America.

Second printing, 1974.

A Note About the Book...

One of many interesting things about the Teton-Yellowstone area is the close proximity of two parks that are so different. Once in the vicinity, it is almost impossible to go to one and not the other. We had originally planned to include trail guides to both areas in a single Totebook, but it was not long before we discovered that it would be difficult—even with two separate volumes—to keep them down to "jean-pocket size." But still, we felt it was unrealistic to deal with each park as a separate island. As a result, we have combined the authors' background information to both guides—*Hiking the Teton Backcountry*, by Paul Lawrence, and its companion volume, *Hiking the Yellowstone Backcountry*, by Orville E. Bach Jr.—into a single introductory section which is included in both volumes. Our thanks to Eugene J. Walter Jr., who worked from the manuscripts and a number of reference books to provide the overview of the two parks. As you read through the text you will find that the geologic history, weather information, and sometimes even the grizzly, do not stop at the boundary of one park, but continue into the other. We thought that you probably would, too.

...And the Author

Paul Lawrence lives in a log cabin at the foot of the Tetons with his wife Ginger, daughter Anthea and son Colin. His writings and photographs have appeared in *Audubon Magazine*, *National Parks Magazine*, *Trail Camping*, *Wilderness Camping*, and *Ski Magazine*. His photographs have been exhibited at the Moose Visitor Center in Grand Teton National Park and at the Rendezvous Gallery in Jackson, Wyoming.

Lawrence is currently at work on a photographic book on the Tetons entitled "Gifts of Life: Seasons in the Tetons."

—the editors
Sierra Club Books

Acknowledgments

I would like to thank Boyd Evison, former Assistant Superintendent of Grand Teton National Park, Management Assistant Tony Bevenetto and Seasonal Naturalist Joe Shellenberger for their help in preparing the material for this book. Their efforts to formulate a new park usage policy to brighten the future of the park have been particularly gratifying. There are many other Park Service personnel who contributed their time trying to answer the often difficult questions posed. My thanks to them as well.

The idea for writing this book was suggested by Connie Stallings of New York City. Without her encouragement it never would have been written.

My wife Ginger typed the manuscript, correcting grammar and foggy thinking, for which I am eternally grateful.

Preface

While a guide book is not a substitute for experience and common sense, I believe this book will give someone in reasonably good shape enough information to hike with confidence in the mountains surrounding Jackson Hole.

Wilderness values are difficult to talk about yet relatively easy to experience. I had some doubts about writing a guide book to an area I love. I do not wish to see the trails crowded and the land overcamped. I finally decided to write the book because I believe that man behaves more responsibly in small groups than large ones.

There are numerous organizations which offer wilderness experiences for a fee. For some people they undoubtedly perform a service, but for others they tend to dilute the power and meaning of the experience. It is my hope that an individual who makes the necessary preparation can meet the challenge of the wilderness alone or in a small group. This guide book is my contribution.

Man returns to the wilderness for many reasons. What point would there be in going if he had all the answers? Perhaps there is some danger involved. For some it might be frightening, especially at night. So be it. It is not for everyone to hear what the wilderness has to say. If you are someone who needs wilderness, go to it soon. It may not be there much longer.

When Thoreau said "In wildness is the preservation of the world," he could not have foreseen how quickly his words would become a desperate cry. In the very near future the battle will be won or lost. We cannot afford to remain uninvolved. The stakes are too high.

—Paul Lawrence
Jackson, Wyoming, 1973

Contents

TRAIL DESCRIPTIONS

Trails are listed from north to south

South Horn of Mount Moran from Leigh Lake

Before You Set Out

*By Eugene J. Walter
with Paul Lawrence*

A Natural History of the Teton-Yellowstone Region

If animals could vote, there would be more places like Grand Teton National Park. Take the ducks, for instance. Flocks of mallards approach the park by riverway, hugging the water, refusing to become airborne targets. Then they reach the boundary. Invisible though that line may be, the birds lift off and fly into the peace they know is on the other side. It is there for us, too.

The land of Yellowstone (3,472 square miles) is mostly high, rolling, forested plateau bounded by mountains—the Gallatin and Madison ranges to the west, the Absarokas along the east. Six miles south of the Yellowstone border is the northernmost entrance to Grand Teton National Park (484 square miles) and the sky-high spires that gave the mountain range its name and a reputation as a climbers' paradise. Most visitors arrive in their 4 wheeled prisons, checking off a list of postcard sights as if they were touring a version of Disneyland. Pity. Because beyond the limited viewpoint of looping scenic roads are thousands of acres of wilderness—enough spectacular scenery to keep even the most dedicated explorers busy for years. It takes time.

It *took* time. Billions of years went into the creation of these unique landscapes. Yet many of the wilderness wonderments you walk among today have been there for only a few ticks on the geologic clock.

The Making of the Mountains

The Tetons are among the youngest mountains in the Rockies—less than 10 million years old (most of the others go back 50 million years). The crystalline peaks gleaming in today's sun had their origin deep under the earth's crust in Precambrian times. During the Early Precambrian, sedimentary and volcanic rock accumulated down there in great heat and under intense pressure. This material was recrystallized into gneiss and schist (or mica schist) and repeatedly folded into enormous, multi-colored layers. As the strata settled, fractures developed. The underground heated up again and volcanic action poured molten streams of pegmatite and pink and light-gray granite up into the cracks, while on the surface, volcanoes and mountains were forming. This mixture ultimately cooled and solidified in those fractures to form cross-hatchings and rocky wriggles called dikes.

Eons passed, and the mountains eroded away to a rolling plain on the earth's surface—until some 600 million years ago when shallow seas swept over the area to deposit the sedimentary rock that still covers much of the range. During the next 500 million years the waters receded and returned periodically, each time leaving behind additional crusty layers of limestone and sandstone. As the climate slowly changed, the region stabilized into luxuriant jungles so that, about 50 million years ago, the area that is now Grand Teton National Park resembled the Florida everglades.

The Tetons began to form in mid-Pliocene. The whole rocky melange that had been brewing for eons began an upward movement. The Teton fault shifted and colossal blocks of gneiss, schist, and granite rose, breaking through the crust of limestone and sandstone that had covered them for centuries. The tilted blocks gradually lifted. Since that time, the forces of erosion have carved the Tetons we see today.

As the rock mass uplifted along the whole 40-mile-long fault, myriad dikes were exposed. Perhaps the most intriguing that are visible today are the enormous, nearly vertical dikes of diabase, shaded from dark green to black. The biggest of these, on Mount Moran, ranges from 100 to 120 feet in thickness and extends 7 miles in length. Grand Teton's black dike is 40 to 60 feet thick and the one on Middle Teton, 20 to 40 feet thick.

Volcanic Activity in Yellowstone

The formation of Yellowstone came somewhat later and with considerably more violence. A series of volcanic eruptions—the first 2 million years ago, the second about 1.2 million years ago—blasted pumice and ash over hundreds of cubic miles. A third cycle of eruptions began 600,000 years ago. Molten rock, or magma, churned upward into underground basins, creating on the surface a dome-like mountain 50 to 75 miles across. As surface stone cracked, some of the lava spilled out across the landscape. Finally, after preliminary rumbling and smoking, a massive explosion of gas spewed tons of debris over the land as far as what is now Kansas and Nebraska, destroying every vestige of life in its path. Modern geologists estimate the force of this blast at 200 times that of Krakatoa, the modern record-holder.

Gas pressure eventually subsided and the flow of molten ash and pumice halted. The giant earth dome that had risen over the lava collapsed and became an elliptical crater, or caldera. The crater, measuring 50 miles in diameter (just short of a world's record) has eroded and become overgrown with vegetation, but is still visible below Mount Washburn.

Volcanic activity continued with leaks rather than blowouts. The material that trickled over the earth—sometimes cutting a path 30 miles across—was mostly rhyolite, a blend of quartz and feldspar that still covers much of Yellowstone. Some of the rhyolite solidified into a black or brown glass known as obsidian. Thus, today's backpacker sometimes finds himself walking over black glass, as on the Shoshone Trail.

Eruptions continued with diminishing force until about 75,000 years ago. Between each of these cycles, trees sprouted in the new volcanic soil, only to be destroyed by the next series of subterranean upheavals. During some of the less violent blasts, nearby trees were buried—and preserved—under clouds of ash, dust, and other debris. Their death was the birth of Yellowstone's 40 square miles of fossil forest—the world's largest. Many of the trees, like some on Specimen Ridge, remain upright, a unique departure from the fallen logs of other petrified forests around the world.

New water courses opened across the land where those early forests were taking root, and a lake welled up inside the giant crater. Its waters spilled over the rim to become the Yellowstone River, which in turn cut a 26 mile gash known as the Grand Canyon of Yellowstone. In one section the river has long been (and still is) heated by magma deep below the surface. The scalding water has boiled the canyon walls for century after century, transforming the brown and gray rhyolite into vivid yellow rock. Hence, Yellowstone.

A Glacial Facelift

It remained for ice to finish the work, giving Yellowstone and Grand Teton their more or less final shape. In the Pleistocene, temperatures dropped, great masses of snow and ice accumulated and, ultimately, enormous glaciers pushed forward and altered the landscape. The glaciers arrived in 3 major and several minor waves over a period extending from 350,000 to 9,000 years ago. Each time, Yellowstone was almost completely submerged under these ice oceans, in some places as deep as 3,000 feet. On several occasions, sheets of ice flowing south from the Yellowstone plateau, met and joined sheets moving from the east into Jackson Hole.

Over these thousands of years, the climate warmed periodically, causing the glaciers to melt and retreat; but when the temperatures dropped, the glaciers returned once more. Each time they left their mark. The ice runoff branched into the canyons, grinding the edges off those chasms and rounding out their floors. Yellowstone's Madison River Canyon was transformed from a sharp cleft into a U-shaped valley. About 30,000 years ago, ice that was several thousand feet thick filled Jackson Hole and gouged out more of the great dip of flat plain that is walled by the towering Tetons. In valley after valley, a combination of glacial battering, frost, and avalanches chiseled gentle slopes into sharp inclines. The same abrasive action sharpened mountain peaks and ridges above.

During the last major advance, approximately 9,000 years ago, glaciers streamed through the Teton valleys, depositing great masses of rock, gravel, sand, and other debris into terminal moraines. When the glaciers eventually melted, these moraines remained as natural dams to form several of the Teton area's major lakes: Jackson, Leigh, Jenny, Bradley, Taggart, and Phelps.

Glaciers are still to be seen in Grand Teton National Park. But they are small, essentially dormant. They are probably recent arrivals, not remnants of the ice monsters that once dominated this part of the earth. Backpackers can hike trails to both Teton and Schoolroom glaciers for a glimpse of the past.

Flora

Of the 2 park areas, Yellowstone is the more heavily wooded. About 80 percent of it is forest, and 80 percent of that is lodgepole pine. Apparently, the lodgepole took over because forest fires were good for them. Up to a point, that is. It takes fiery heat to pry open the cones the lodgepole deposits on the ground. The cones can then eject their seeds for sprouting. While fire wiped out other tree species, it helped the lodgepole to reproduce and move in where the others had fallen.

Conifers are now dominant in both parks, but no one is sure how most of the trees and plants got to this region. The experts think that at least some of the species traveled a circuitous route, riding the breeze and the glaciers.

A trek through the wild places of present-day Yellowstone and Grand Teton is like an excursion through a series of gardens, the more charming for their lack of formality. You can meander over a meadowland trail edged with a blue and purplish bouquet of larkspur, lupine, gentian, and elephanthead, patches of cinquefoil and buttercups, and fields of lilies sprinkled with sage. A wooded path will lead you past trees garlanded with pale lavendar clematis, stands of tall monkshood and blue harebells, starry asters, and brilliant fireweed. Luminescent mosses cloak the rocky banks of a mountain stream and, under an archway of shady alders, the soft earth yields a colorful congregation of pink monkeyflowers, scarlet paintbrush, mountain bluebell, ivory columbine, red and yellow coralroot, yellow senecio. If you want to be sure of the name of that blossom beside the trail, take along a field guide to flowers.

Fauna

Man has always been lured to the Teton-Yellowstone region more by animals than by anything else. Ancestors of many of today's wild species probably arrived via the land bridge that once spanned the Bering Strait to Asia. During the Ice Age, primitive hunters followed the mammoth to this area. Later, the Indians pursued bison, elk, and deer along the slopes and through the valleys. The first full-time human residents we know of were mountaineering Indians who stalked bighorn sheep. The earliest white men were obsessed with the beaver whose luxurious fur made it a natural resource to be exploited.

Most people today regard this part of the world as bear country. Small wonder. The black bear is the only sizable animal most people are likely to see. Then there are the others the tourists have no desire to meet: the grizzlies. Actually, there are only about 250 spread around Yellowstone (each requires a lot of space) and a mere handful south of the park in the Teton Wilderness. Fierce and fearless, the grizzly has all the equipment necessary to be king in these parts: bone-crushing jaws, razor-sharp, 6 inch claws, and amazing speed for a bulky, lumbering, 600 pound animal. There is nothing subtle about a grizzly bear, yet there is nothing quite so winsome as the springtime sight of a grizzly leading her cubs across Yellowstone's Hayden Valley in a search for roots and berries.

The grasslands are home to the elk, or wapiti, most numerous of the region's large animals. The smaller mule deer is also here, grazing the valleys and forest edges. The pronghorn, America's only antelope, prefers the plains but occasionally ventures into open slopes of the valleys. Seeing one for more than a few seconds may take some doing since they are as speedy as they are skittish.

Moose, the only other really large creatures hereabouts, are to be found mostly in the wetlands, occasionally feeding along hillsides. Look for them on the Yellowstone River downstream from Yellowstone Lake, or at Avalanche Canyon in the Tetons. Marshlands also supply food and nesting grounds for the North American trumpeter swan. Like the bison, these birds were once on the verge of extinction. Only 70 remained at one point but, given protection, they have come back to number in the thousands. Mountain marshes, ponds, and lakes are home as well to the muskrat, mink, otter, beaver, sandhill crane, great blue heron, osprey, and a variety of ducks, geese, and coots.

Any visit to the park interior is a birdwatcher's delight. More than 200 species have been identified. Warblers, juncos, kingfishers, nuthatches, goldfinches, flycatchers, swallows, hummingbirds, tanagers, chickadees. . . . This is another cataloguing operation that is better done on foot with the help of a pocket-sized field guide.

Park animals are protected from man but not from each other. The aim now is to give equal rights to predators and restore the balance of life. An earlier misguided policy held that eliminating predators would be good for the deer. It wasn't. Deer herds became over-populated, which nearly starved them out. It isn't nice to fool around with Mother Nature.

The unjustly maligned coyote patrols valleys, mountains, forests, meadows, or marshes keeping things tidy. If it weren't for coyotes, the parks would be overrun with mice, gophers, and rabbits. Smaller carnivorous critters—red fox, lynx, mink, wolverine, badger—are a secretive lot, difficult, but not impossible to spot. There are not many wolves or mountain lions and they, too, are shy about meeting people. With good reason.

Weather

Month to month, the climate is rather similar in Yellowstone and Grand Teton; but the latter generally takes you to higher elevations. The town of Jackson is 6,234 feet above sea level. In the Tetons you will be spending much of your time well above 10,000 feet. Some trails are closed by snow for all but a few weeks of the year.

No matter what it's doing in Yellowstone, the Tetons are big enough to produce their own weather spectaculars. And, being so big, they are also capable of hiding from the hiker the delights they are brewing, until suddenly—it's there. Snow in July. Sixty-mile-an-hour winds gusting between the peaks during thunderstorms. Lightning zapping the slopes, and clouds of needle-like sleet, and hailstones as big and as hard as golf balls—all apparently aimed at your head. Once you've passed the timberline, there are few places to hide. Even after clear, sunny days, the nighttime temperature at these heights dips close to freezing.

June

Each month has its advantages and disadvantages. If the high country is your goal, better wait till midsummer. Winter weather persists above 6,500 feet through May. June is still wintry above 8,500 feet. At slightly lower elevations, the bulk of the wilderness is frequently too soggy to do extensive hiking for at least the first 3 weeks of June. Slushy snow and high water make it inaccessible.

June can be ideal for traveling the shorter trails of the 2 parks. Newly blossoming wildflowers line paths through the valleys. Waterfalls, refreshed by melting snows, are at the peak of their beauty. The mountains are still capped with white. Most of the migratory birds are back and there's a flurry of nest building. Mule deer fawns are usually born in June. It's easier to see wildlife in general. Perhaps the best reason for going is that few tourists have arrived. June is wonderfully unpredictable. Every day of your visit could be clear and sunny. It might rain every day. It could snow.

July

July is more inviting to the backpacker. Days are generally brighter, brisk, seldom chilly. Nights are cold, particularly in the Tetons. In the mountains there are thunderstorms and stiff winds almost every afternoon; sometimes snow. But it should all pass in 1 or 2 hours. Patience.

When the water goes down late in July, fishing is at its best. Wildflowers are blooming at higher elevations. As the weather warms, some of the wildlife retreats up the slopes to mountain meadows. There are still many elk in the river valleys and moose in the bogs. The pelicans and gulls on the Molly Islands are scooping up fish for their newborn chicks. This is the month when fledglings of almost every bird species try their wings, and the trumpeter swans lead their young to water.

July is also the time when the bugs wake up. There are clouds of mosquitoes around marshes, lakes, meadows; any place where the snow has just melted. And they bite and bite and bite. Colder temperatures make them inactive. So they rest up at night for the next day's feast. If the mosquitoes neglect any part of you, an assortment of other insects are ready to help. It's imperative that you carry the proper repellent, creams, clothing, and netting for your tent.

August

In many ways, August is the prime month for backpacking excursions. Weather is dependable except for occasional thundershowers, especially high in the Tetons. Days are hot, nights are refreshingly cool, sometimes cold. The snow is gone, the water has receded, trails are in great shape. The mosquitoes and their pestiferous brethren have subsided considerably. Above the timberline, alpine vegetation flowers briefly. In the forests, young birds declare their independence of the nest.

September and Later

For many backpackers, September is the *only* time for Yellowstone and Grand Teton. Wildflowers are disappearing but the trees are touched with color. Scarlets and golds appear on the high slopes and seem to drift down toward the valleys as the month goes on. The groves of aspen acquire their golden glow.

Ponds and lakes are filled with ducks and geese stopping over on their way south. Flocks of songbirds pause here on their migrations. The insects are gone. So are most of the people.

The big game is at its best. The ones that moved into the mountains for the summer are returning to the valleys. Deer, elk, and moose are living trophies, their racks of antlers matured to magnificence, their coats thick as they glisten with a new sheen in the autumn sunlight. For the elk, this is the time of the rut or mating season. The bull elk announces his intentions by bugling a high, piercing shriek that descends to a booming, low grunt—a sound you won't forget.

In September, the wilderness is wild. So is the weather, which becomes unpredictable. Rain is common, snow is likely. But, while caution is necessary with snow, it isn't quite the same hazard as early in the season because it hasn't had time to accumulate in great depths. In the Tetons, September and October are good hiking months. A small amount of new snow falls in October, but it usually isn't enough to present obstacles.

Clothing and Equipment

Your Wilderness Wardrobe

Underfoot: For day hikes over relatively smooth, well-traveled trails, a light trail shoe is sufficient. But, where you will encounter rocky terrain, snow and ice, a heavy boot is advisable. Whatever the weight, certain specifications are in order:

- Sturdy, rock-resistant leather throughout.
- Rubber lug soles.
- Reinforced heel and toe.
- Protective padding of soft leather around the ankle for support, warmth, and comfort. (Be sure there's enough room for heavy socks inside.)
- A long, padded tongue.
- Waterproofing. (Remember to re-waterproof between backpacking expeditions.)

Once you have the boots, break them in gradually. Wear them around the house; take walks outdoors. Always wear the kind of socks you're taking on the trip. The boots are broken in when you can walk all day with a full pack over all kinds of terrain without sore feet. Clearly, this isn't something you wait to do until 2 days before the trip.

If your projected route includes streams without bridges, it's advisable to have an extra pair of lightweight shoes handy: sneakers or mukluks. A change before fording saves your boots and keeps your feet dry. Before you bed down for the night, remember to turn your boots upside-down to keep the moisture out.

Inside the boots, traditionalists prefer good old heavy woolen socks—warm and cushiony. You may want a light cotton inner-sock if they're scratchy. New terry stitched socks made of synthetic fiber and cotton can equal wool in warmth and cushioning. The air pockets in the looser weave also insulate better, keep feet dryer, and eliminate the need for inner socks. Terry stitched thermal socks are available in wool.

Inside: You may find yourself a bit less fastidious in the wilderness, but, if you insist on changing underwear every day, accept the fact that you'll have to do more laundry along the trail. Three extra sets is ample. Consider taking a set of long johns (cotton or wool).

Outside: Wear warm, long pants made of wool or cotton twill. Be sure the legs fit loosely. Tight legs get hot and bind up; awful if they get wet. Walking shorts—also loose-fitting—are a nice option when the weather heats up.

You'll probably want to spend most of the day in a cotton or light wool shirt. For cooler temperatures you'll need something more. Wool sweaters are not such a hot idea. They are too bulky and they don't offer enough options to adjust for changing temperatures. A heavy wool shirt or a light down jacket is better. A good wool sheds water and stays warm even when wet, but it adds weight and bulk. A zippered nylon/down jacket insulates well and lets moisture escape; it's light and compressible. However, if it should get soaked, it takes a long time to dry out. For early and late in the season, a heavier down jacket is recommended.

Take wool mittens and a cap if you're going early or late in the season. A hat will protect you from rain, cold and sun.

A poncho is the world's greatest portable shelter and one of the most essential items on your list. If you're caught in heavy rains or wicked winds, you can poke your head through the center, drape the big waterproof rectangle over you and either wait till the weather blows over or flap along the trail like a big bat. Your poncho does multiple duty: a rain fly for your tent, an emergency tent along the trail, a ground cloth, a cover for your sleeping bag on extra misty nights. Spend the money for a poncho made of tough, lightweight nylon coated with plastic resin. The inexpensive sheet-plastic variety won't hold up through many trips. Get one big enough to cover your pack frame as well as yourself (100 by 70 inches).

Backpacks

On day hikes, you can use a summit pack or rucksack. For a longer trip, you should have a pack mounted on a metal frame. Magnesium frames are becoming more popular than aluminum because magnesium is lighter yet just as strong. Make sure the frame is the right length to fit comfortably on your torso. It should curve along your spine. Get one with a padded waist belt and test it with a loaded pack. A proper frame will hold the load high so the weight is directed down through your hips to your legs. Padded shoulder straps are more comfortable.

The best packs are made of waterproof, nylon duck. The easiest to organize have strips of fabric inside that divide the pack into vertical or horizontal compartments. Look

for plenty of zippered pockets on the outside to stow maps
and other small items you want to get at quickly.

Sleeping Bags

In this part of the world, any summer night can be cold.
The lightweight summer sleeping bag that kept you cozy in
the Catskills will not serve you so well out west. The mini-
mum you should figure on for Yellowstone and Grand
Teton is a bag that will keep you warm in 30°F. That
should suffice for the latter part of June through most of
August. From mid-May to mid-June and the last week of
August to mid-September you will need a bag for 20°F.
Earlier or later, a 10°F. bag is necessary. These are general
standards. What you choose naturally depends on your own
ability to adjust to cold. For the sake of long-range flexibility, it may make sense to get the 10°F. bag (for which
you will pay more). Unzipped, it can be comfortable up to
60°F. When it's warmer than that, you can open the bag
over you like a blanket instead of crawling inside.

The critical element in your comfort is the guts of the
bag: the filler. The one that offers the best combination of
insulation, light weight, and compactness is goose down, an
excellent insulator. Its fluffiness traps warm air more effi-
ciently than any other filler. Duck down and synthetic
foam (bulky but light) are reasonable compromises.

The factor that contributes most to warmth is the "loft"
of the down, meaning the thickness of the sleeping bag
after you fluff it out and lay it on a flat surface. That
thickness creates insulating power. A 6 inch loft is proper
for a bag that has a 10°F. rating. The finest quality goose
down is the most expensive because it holds its loft longer
than the cheaper grades. Warm toes are worth almost any

price. Figure on spending $80 or more for a good quality goose down bag.

The other major considerations in your choice of a bag are lightness (4 pound maximum) and outer material (get tightly woven, water-repellent, rip-stop nylon). The exact type of construction is not vital so long as the down is spread evenly through the bag by a series of baffles, or tubes, sewn around the circumference of the bag (not lengthwise). Without the baffles, the down will shift and settle in one spot. Style is a matter of personal preference. The mummy bag with its hood is the snuggest. If that's too confining for you, get a semi-rectangular bag that spreads out more.

Having invested in a good sleeping bag, take good care of it. Put something between it and the ground, or it will soak up moisture. It dries *very* slowly. Freshen it with sun and air every morning before you repack. For added comfort you may want to bring a foam pad to put under your sleeping bag.

Tents

In this region a tent is not a luxury. Heavy rain, snow, sleet, and high winds can occur with little warning. Obviously, you want a tent that burdens you as little as possible, while supplying maximum protection. A 2-man tent shouldn't add more than 5 pounds to your load. Figure 8 pounds as the maximum for a 3-man shelter.

Tents constructed with a double layer of coated nylon are more expensive than those made with a single layer. Moisture condenses on the tent *inside* the single layer and drips, turning your sleeping quarters into a shower. Double layer tents are made with 2 sheets of fabric sewn together so that the moisture trickles down the outer layer, not on you. Your tent should be equipped with completely enclosed mosquito netting. That, too, adds to the cost.

In midsummer at lower elevations, you can usually get by with a minimal tent. The tube tent, a thin, 9 foot polyethelene tube, is available in 1- or 2-man sizes. You can also use a tarp. Take about 50 feet of braided nylon parachute cord to string up your tent. If your tarp doesn't have grommets, you'll need clamps. Tubes and tarps will keep out the rain, but they present no barrier to mosquitoes or biting flies. High winds can demolish them. In the high country, they are totally inadequate.

Filling Your Pack

Some of the items that belong in your pack don't fit into a category.

- Sunglasses. (Essential above timberline and in snow and ice. Sunlight becomes intensely bright in the clear, thin air.)
- Suntan lotion.
- Lip salve.
- Insect repellent.
- Swiss army knife.
- Small flashlight. (No telling what you'll have to find in the dark. It can also be used for emergency signalling. Tape the switch when it's in your pack so it doesn't turn on.)
- Toothbrush. (A little box of bicarbonate of soda is lighter, more compact, and more effective than toothpaste. A small spool of dental floss will also keep your teeth from rotting. Or carve yourself a tooth-

pick from a twig.)

- Soap. (Not detergent. Liquid biodegradeable. In a plastic squeezebottle with a leak-proof spout. Use that soap for every cleaning job.)
- Toilet paper. (Unrolled from the tube and rerolled flat and tight. Keep it in a plastic bag. Use it sparingly.)
- Plastic bags. (For lots of things that crop up, including the garbage you take out.)
- Canteen. (Not an absolute necessity. In this region running water is generally not far away.)
- Compass.
- First aid kit.
- Ice Axe. (In the Tetons many of the trails are covered by steep snowfields that bottom out in boulder fields. It is foolhardy to attempt crossing at those points without an ice axe. It is equally foolhardy to carry the axe when you haven't mastered the technique of using one. If you lack previous experience, plan to spend several days at one of the local mountaineering schools. If that is more bother than you bargained for, the Jenny Lake Ranger Station will provide information about trails that are free of snow-swept crossing points. Locations vary from year to year because the snow pack varies. But any hiker who wishes to gain access to the beauties of the high country must be skilled with an ice axe.)

Optional:

- Small terrycloth face towel.
- Comb or hairbrush. (No telling who you'll meet on

the trail.)
- ● Candle. (In case the flashlight breaks, and for lighting stoves.)
- ● Binoculars.

Now that you have all the equipment you *want*, eliminate everything you *don't need*. If you're new at this, even packing may require some practice.

Food

Fires in the backcountry are dangerous and illegal. If you want to cook you will need a stove. Compact butane-cartridge stoves, like the Bleuet, are easy to operate. Gasoline stoves—the Svea, the Optimus—are better in cold weather, but it takes priming, pumping, and a certain amount of hokus pokus to light one.

Your kitchen:
- 1½ or 2 quart pot. The lid can double as a frying pan or plate.
- Plastic or metal cup.
- Spoon.
- Bowl for mixing or eating (optional).
- Bottle to mix powdered drinks.
- Spatula if fried foods are on the menu.
- Scouring pads for clean-up.
- Waterproof stick-matches in a waterproof container.

Breakfast: Remember what your mother told you: eat a good breakfast. Her advice was never truer than on the trail. For juice, Tang is the best blend of taste and economy. Orange and tomato juice crystals taste good but cost much more. To warm yourself, freeze-dried or instant coffee, or instant cocoa is good. Mixed together, they make a pleasant

mocha drink. Powdered milk is another one of those compromises you accept in backpacking. Milkman is more pal-
atable than most brands because a small amount of cream is
added to it. Perma-Pak is the richest. You can even reconsti-
tute it as cream. Both brands are packaged in convenient 1
quart containers. Remember to take sugar.

On cold mornings instant oatmeal or other hot cereals
make a nutritious meal. Granola is filling in the stomach
but heavy in the pack. Raisins, dates, and various freeze-
dried fruits flavor up any cereal, hot or cold.

Freeze-dried eggs are an enormous improvement over the
old-fashioned powdered eggs. Wilson's bacon bar is an excellent source of protein. Jerky (dried beef) is an equally
good protein supplier.

Lunch: As a foundation for most trail lunches, depend on
jerky and gorp, that unfortunately named but highly palat-
able and nutritious blend of raisins, seeds, dried fruits, nuts,
and chocolate.

You can vary your lunches with hard cheese and un-
sliced salami. (On lengthy trips, salami may get a little ripe.)
Try breads and crackers such as Mount Logan Bread and
Pilot Biscuits. Canned butter (Darigold) will keep without
refrigeration. Or spread your bread with dehydrated cheese
or peanut butter. Dehydrated salads are available: tuna,
potato, or egg.

Wash it all down with tea or lemonade or other fruit
drinks. Wyler's fruit-ades are generally favored. Pem bars are
a good finish to a lunch. If you'd rather have chocolate,
Hershey's tropical bar won't melt.

Dinner: Soup helps to replace liquid you've lost during the day. It's also nourishing and takes the chill off the evening.

There are many possibilities for the main course with today's wide variety of freeze-dried entrees. Wilson's meat bar weighs 3 ounces. No refrigeration or cooking is necessary. Dice it and add to vegetables, noodles, or rice for a quick, tasty mulligan stew. Mountain House beef patties, pork patties, and meat balls are ready 1 minute after you add boiling water. (They are packed in cans which you should take out with you.) Avoid steaks and pork chops. They are too difficult to rehydrate thoroughly, and you'll have to carry a frying pan and oil to cook them. There is an extensive variety of freeze-dried and dehydrated vegetables and desserts.

Many people enjoy harvesting fruit that grows along the trail at various times during the summer: blueberries, huckleberries, raspberries, serviceberries, thimbleberries. It means expending extra time and energy but, if you find them, they make delightful desserts and delicious additions to breakfast. Know what you're picking. Not every bright berry is edible.

Snacks: This is one time you *should* nibble between meals. Your nibbles should have food value to supply extra protein, recharge your energy quickly (with easily assimilated sugars), and to replenish water you've lost through perspiration.

The ever-popular gorp is your most likely trail food. Also helpful: nuts, dried fruits, seeds, fruit sticks, hard candy, and drink mixes.

The feeding schedules you normally follow go out the door when you do. In the wilderness eat when you're hungry.

At all times throughout the day, drink plenty liquids. During the hottest part of the summer, a supply of salt tablets is advisable. Nutritional needs are an individual thing. If you have any doubts, talk to your doctor. A small container of multi-vitamin capsules or vitamin C capsules might be in order.

In General . . . Any dish that needs more than 30 minutes of preparation should be left behind. The repeated emphasis on speed is especially pertinent on trips to Yellowstone and the Tetons. The higher you go, the lower the boiling point of water. When you hit 8,000 feet, it takes twice as long to cook as it does at sea level. Remember also that food digests more slowly at high altitudes. Frequent meals are better than a lot at once.

Plan ahead. If you average out to a pound or a pound-and-a-half of dry food for each day, you're on target. Become a food packager. Pack each item in the quantity desired for each meal. Many main courses are already packed in suitable single-meal containers.

Don't forget the salt and pepper.

Maps

Among all the paraphernalia you're taking, no item is more important than a map. For your present purposes you want a United States Geological Survey topographic map, popularly called a "topo."

The U.S.G.S. topos pinpoint trails, roads, contours, elevations, drainages, water courses, lakes, meadows, forests, valleys, and man-made additions to the area. The most accurately detailed are the 7½-minute maps (minutes of latitude and longitude).

You can order topographic maps directly from the United States Geological Survey, Distribution Center, in Denver, Colorado 80225. Fifteen-minute quads sell for 50¢, the full park maps for $1.50. If you are unsure about what maps you will need, write to U.S.G.S. for a free index to topographic maps of Wyoming. In addition, they publish a free booklet that will instruct you in the mysteries of interpreting topographic maps. You can also purchase U.S.G.S. topographic maps at park visitor centers and at local outdoor equipment stores.

The U.S.G.S. quads are usually reliable, but not infallible. Don't be upset if what appears on the map doesn't match what is in front of you. You will still have to use common sense.

Other pathfinders:

Aerial photographs of the area are available from the Regional Engineer, Rocky Mountain Region, at the U.S.G.S. in Denver. Same address. Ask for a free index to aerial photography. From that, you can order the photo indices you need. Price: $2.50 each.

The United States Forest Service publishes several types of maps. Some of them are free: fold-out maps of Teton National Forest, Teton Wilderness, and Targhee National Forest (which is adjacent to the Tetons). Larger scale (1 mile to ¼ inch) maps of Teton National Forest and the eastern division of Targhee National Forest are available for $1.00. For both types of maps, contact the United States Department of Agriculture, Forest Service, Federal Office Building, 324 25th Street, Ogden, Utah 84401. The Teton National Forest headquarters in Jackson can also supply you with maps of their domain. You can obtain a free map of the state by writing to the Wyoming Travel Commission, Cheyenne, Wyoming 82001.

Cameras

In high mountain country there are sharp lighting contrasts. Forests are full of shadows. Use a light meter, preferably one that measures spot as well as average readings. Snow and ice will fool your meter into giving readings that are wrong for your subject. Open the diaphragm 2 stops more than the meter indicates in order to compensate for glare. Above timberline there is so much sky that the extra light will confuse your meter. For more realistic readings, aim the meter more toward the ground than you normally would. If your camera has a through-the-lens meter, that device will do the job, but it lacks the flexibility—and probably the accuracy—of a separate meter. When you depend on an attached meter, you stand a better chance of getting the photo you want if you bracket the shot with several exposures.

You won't need filters for color film. It's always worthwhile to keep a skylight filter over your lens to protect it against scratches. Use a medium yellow filter if you're shooting black and white.

In this sort of country, a wide-angle lens is generally the most useful, particularly in the vicinity of the high peaks and deep canyons. New panoramas present themselves every time you look in another direction. For a 35mm camera, a 28mm or even a 21mm lens is advisable. A 35mm lens doesn't expand the scope of your camera much more than its standard 50mm.

Ninety mm or 135mm telephoto lenses rank next in terms of usefulness. Great for capturing details of the scenic wonders around you. A 200mm lens will certainly help, but without a tripod you need a pretty steady hand, or a shoulder brace. A conveniently positioned rock with a fairly level surface will also do, but don't count on one always being where you want it. Any lens with a focal length longer than 200mm definitely requires a tripod, and probably a cable release. (Strictly for serious wildlife photographers. The opportunities are sensational *if* you're willing to lug the extra weight.)

Nature buffs interested in closeups of wildflowers and butterflies might also consider macro lenses. Particularly those with a focal length longer than 50mm.

There are even some situations where the normal 50mm lens that came with your camera is the most sutiable. For almost every occasion on this backpacking excursion, you will be well prepared if you take along a wide-angle, a normal, and a medium telephoto. If 3 is too many, take a wide-angle and a telephoto.

For the camera buff there is no such thing as too much film. Allow at least a roll a day. It takes a lot of shooting— even for professionals—to come up with a few really superb pictures.

The abundance of lighting variables raises questions about what kind of color film to take. A medium-speed film should handle most situations you're likely to encounter. It gives you more latitude in dark forests and handles all lighting with more color warmth than high-speed film.

Fishing

The pristine waters of Yellowstone and Grand Teton—lakes, rivers, streams, ponds, brooks—offer some of the most spectacular trout fishing in the American West. Sport species include cutthroat (named for the red mark on its jaw), rainbow, brown, brook, and lake (also called mackinaw) trout.

A policy of artificial stocking has been abandoned, but the damage has been done. To a person whose primary interest is the quality of the fishing—it is terrific—"damage" may seem like a peculiar word; and the question of native versus introduced species may appear to be over-concern with ecological esthetics. But, if a wilderness is to remain truly wild, it must be maintained in its original state with minimal meddling by man. Native fish that were interesting in their own right, both as battlers and as food, are fewer. Their decline has forced the adoption of stringent regulations on park fishing so that what remains may be preserved. There may be many cutthroat trout, but they are not there simply for humans to consume. Numerous other creatures—the grizzly, otter, mink, pelican, osprey, kingfisher, heron, and others—all prey on this fish: It is a vital link in the ecosystem. It has been estimated that pelicans alone —most of them from the Molly Islands colony—consume up to *400,000* cutthroat each year.

Safety

The wilderness naturally presents some hazards, but traveling through the backcountry is not a perilous venture—if you use your head. To a large extent, safety is common sense and logic.

Before You Go

Stop at the park ranger station before you take off into the wilderness. The rangers there will issue you a backcountry use permit (no charge). Permits have become necessary as more and more people are attracted to the wilderness. Such a system might seem overly restrictive at first, but it is necessary to prevent overuse and overcrowding in the backcountry. Without it, much wilderness would be destroyed. It's for your own benefit.

It's also for your safety. When you obtain permits for a series of campsites you are, in effect, filing an itinerary. Park personnel are then aware of your whereabouts should an emergency develop. Be sure to follow your planned itinerary as closely as possible.

Before leaving, discuss your trip plans with one of the rangers. He'll fill you in on current conditions, warn you away from areas that are, at that moment, dangerous or otherwise unappealing, and supply you with a variety of helpful tips. Aside from your traveling companions, the park rangers are the best friends you have in the wilderness.

The ranger will also provide you with a pamphlet containing backcountry rules and regulations. They are the outgrowth of decades of park management and all of them are designed to protect both you and the park. Don't flout them—violators will be fined by a United States Magistrate.

There may be a few other items of special business between you and the rangers. If canoeing or boating is on your agenda, you'll need a boat permit. The use of firearms is prohibited on most parklands. Should you have any in your possession, you're required to declare them as soon as you enter the park.

The Park Service has designated a set number of backcountry campsites and permits are issued only for those locations. With few exceptions, they are issued on a first-come, first-served basis. If the sites in an area are filled for a particular night, no more permits are given out.

Brief junkets are a good alternative if there are no permits left for the area you want to explore on the day you would like to leave. Even though your primary goal may be a deep penetration of the interior, short hikes act as a sort of decompression chamber from the "civilization" you've left behind. If, like most people, you are an urban dweller, you probably screen out much of the world around you. Some short hiking can help you slow down, open your lungs, tune up your deadened sensitivity, and make you aware of the sights and scents and textures of the natural universe. A day trip or two helps you to get the "feel" of the land, work up to the big plunge.

Don't wait until you're half way up a mountain to open your map. You should familiarize yourself with it and the trail descriptions in this book before you leave.

You are going to find that distances shown on the map are no indication of how long it will take to get from point A to point B. You will also find that climbing steep trails above 7,000 feet with a heavy pack on your back is a slower process than you had imagined. Don't exhaust yourself by trying to travel too far or too fast. Backpacking is a *leisure* activity. A slow, steady, measured pace is preferable to short bursts of speed followed by long rests. Rest when you feel the need, but try not to dally more than 10 minutes each time. Lunchtime should be your long break.

After You Get Lost

There is more to following a trail than looking for markers. At high elevations—particularly in Grand Teton—there are numerous landmarks to help guide you. Above timberline, Jackson Hole is clearly visible and you can always pick out the high peaks of the Tetons, as well as the Gros Ventres, Absaroka, and Snake River ranges. Use them as points of reference in conjunction with your map. To be a successful hiker you should always be aware of significant landmarks. Know where you've been and where you're heading.

Do *not* leave designated trails unless you're a *very experienced hiker*. Cross-country travel can be rewarding, but only if you know what you're doing. Even if you do, you *must* be given permission to travel off established trails, and the use permit you carry must indicate those plans.

Almost any trail can become difficult to follow at times. If it does, stop to consider the rate of climb or descent that it has been following. Most trails are pretty consistent. Yours will almost certainly continue at the same up or down rate that it has been maintaining. To relocate it, move along the same contour you were following without making any major changes in your elevation.

Vegetation may be hiding the trail. Push the underbrush aside and check for human and animal tracks on the ground.

When you reach an unmarked trail junction, take the fork that most closely follows the grade and general direction of the trail you've been following. If you're still doubtful, hunt for footprints. You want the fork that shows the most signs of human traffic, not animals. Most unmarked junctions occur at points where hiking paths are intersected by outfitter and game trails. The latter can be identified by the fact that they follow much steeper grades, and the route tends to be a straight line rather than one which moves along contours. Because such trails may be heavily traveled by horses and other animals, they can give you the idea that they are the most used and, therefore, the most desirable to follow. Don't be misled. Search for signs of other hikers and follow them.

Any one of the above strategies should have you back on the proper trail within a quarter-mile or so.

If you do get to a point where you find yourself saying, "I am lost, hopelessly lost," the first thing to do is: do nothing. Sit down. Reconnoiter. Reconstruct your previous movements on the topo map and find your general location. The solution to your problem will probably become obvious. In any case, don't rush around frantically—you will get more lost, if that's possible. Plan first, then act.

Look for water. Small streams eventually flow into larger ones which parallel trails or roads. All major drainages eventually lead back to civilization. In the Tetons, they all lead to Jackson Hole.

Remember, also, that trails were laid out with a reasonable amount of logic. Though there are many acres in the parks, there are many trails criss-crossing them.

Watching Your Step

There are certain areas and certain times that require extra caution. Be wary of loose rock. Never travel at night or in a blinding storm. When a storm pounces and lightning is suddenly striking nearby peaks, try to leave the area. If you get caught above timberline, avoid exposed ledges or caves. Keep low and remove metal objects, such as your pack and climbing hardware. Use your boot soles as insulation between you and the ground—squat, don't sit.

Backcountry trails frequently ford fairly large streams. Often the current is swift. It's treacherous early in the season when the waterways are swollen by melting snow. The rocks are slippery. Keep shoes on when you're crossing, but remove your socks. Wet socks can cause blisters. If you can find a fallen branch nearby, it could be helpful as a supporting staff. Unfasten the waist strap of your pack to give yourself freedom of movement should you fall. Feel your way across with great deliberation. Keep your eyes on the opposite bank and move slowly. Don't lift your feet. Your balance becomes shakier and the current can upend you.

Blisters and Burns

Blisters are the most common complaint requiring first aid on a hike. The possibility of developing them can be minimized if you do a thorough job of breaking in your shoes before you begin. At the *first* sign of rubbing or tenderness, place some molefoam over the sore areas. If you wait too long, a blister will form. If one does develop, don't apply the molefoam directly over it. Cut a hole in the molefoam to fit the size and shape of the blister and place it around the area. At the end of the day, check the amount of fluid in the blister. If there's a lot, sterilize a needle with a match, prick the blister and drain it. Cover it with a band-aid.

Ticks can be a problem on early summer hikes. Take the time to thoroughly check for them on your body each night in camp. If you find one imbedded in your skin, a little alcohol applied to the spot should send him packing. When there is no alcohol handy, a steady hand holding a burning match near the spot serves the same purpose.

Sunburn can be much more of a problem at high altitudes than at sea level. Apply suntan lotion or glacier cream (near snow and ice) frequently. Use sun screen if you're particularly susceptible. A wide-brimmed hat will protect your nose and ears.

Your first aid kit should include:

- Molefoam or moleskin.
- Needle.
- Band-aids (large, medium, small).
- Alcohol (optional).

Obviously that won't take care of serious injuries, but for the commonplace, you have everything else you need in your pack. Clean handkerchiefs or bandannas can serve as bandages. Soap cleans minor wounds. Water purification tablets aren't necessary in this wilderness.

The Animals

One of the best reasons for trekking through the wilderness is to see the wildlife, yet animals are one of the main reasons more people don't go. The wild beasts that roam here should not be feared so much as they should be respected.

Know their capabilities and their habits. Be prepared.

Respect is one key word in your relationship with wild animals; distance is another. That applies even to the smaller creatures. It may seem perfectly innocuous to feed a seed to a little chipmunk, until he nips you. Next thing you know, you've got a case of tularemia or rabies.

The most dangerous animal you are actually liable to meet is a moose. They are powerful and speedy; they have nasty dispositions, and depending on the time of year, they can be very aggressive. If a moose is headed your way, give him the right of way. Any moose lying down in your path should be given a wide berth. The time to be watchful is midmorning to late afternoon. Be especially wary during the rutting season (early fall) or any time you are in the vicinity of females with calves. Should a moose charge you, run, but don't attempt to outrun him over a level stretch. Climb a tree, or get behind a big rock or a fallen tree. Elk tend to move away when you approach. Don't try to get too close, particularly if they have young with them.

There are so few wolves and mountain lions in the region you would need a lot of luck to see one. You will probably see coyotes, but they will run from you. Tales of attacks on humans by any of these predators are popular mythology. Verified reports are virtually nonexistent.

Don't feed or pester any park animals, from bears to chipmunks. Not just because they might bite, but because they become dependent on these handouts. Comes winter, the tourists disappear, and many of them starve because they have forgotten how to fend for themselves. Respect the animals. Keep your distance.

Backcountry Etiquette

One of the things you must bring with you is your manners. There was a time when wilderness explorers could be casual about matters like garbage and campfires. That time is past. More and more people are crowding into the backcountry. A few thoughtless ones can spoil it for everyone. The wilderness is fragile.

When you are looking for a campsite, find a *naturally* level spot for your sleeping bag and tent. There's no need to shovel or flatten earth. Don't dig a trench around your tent. The scars you leave would take years to heal. Beavers are the only engineers allowed to practice here.

No one relishes the idea of drinking somebody else's bathwater. Remember that when you are washing yourself, your kitchen utensils, or anything else. Don't use soap directly in any of the lakes, pools, streams, or other natural running waters. Don't rinse anything in them. Fill a cookpot with water and carry it away from the stream to do all your bathing and camp clean-up. Make sure you tote it some distance away from the stream so that when you empty the dirty water it doesn't drain back. Be not a polluter of wild waters.

A toilet is the only thing you are allowed to dig in the wilderness and, if you do it right, nobody should know but you. Nature's own disposal system is at your service. Biological action within the top 6 to 8 inches of soil decomposes organic materials.

Carry out all garbage; cans, bottles, plastics, aluminum foil, etc. Burying won't do. Eventually your trash will be unearthed by sharp-nosed animals, or frost action, and the campsite will turn into a garbage dump. Flatten all cans and drop them into one of the plastic sacks you brought along. The containers you packed in full, will weigh a lot less as you pack them out empty.

No dogs, cats, or pet monkeys allowed on any trail in the parks, not even if you have them on a leash. Bears and other native beasts do not like domestic pets. And it's *their* park.

Regulations in the Park and the Forests

On the Trail

Don't take shortcuts across switchbacks. It only accelerates erosion and scars the land forever. Don't discard any cigarettes or matches unless they are 100 percent out. Field-strip your butts. Smokey the Bear is watching you. Don't roll or throw rocks down mountains or into canyons. Somebody might be down there. Don't toss objects into springs, pools, or vents. Don't pick the wildflowers. Don't collect souvenirs. All the above are subject to fines.

Pack animals have the right of way on trails. (If you are planning a backcountry trip by horseback, write in advance to the Chief Ranger's Office in the park. Ask for a copy of current regulations and a list of campsites approved for horse parties.)

You are not allowed to operate motorized vehicles on the trails or in any area of the park that isn't a proper roadway or parking area. Nor can you ride a bicycle on the hiking trails.

The current off-trail registration program will be replaced with signs at the trailheads saying "High Country Trails Dangerous. Check at Ranger Station." It is always advisable to register so that the Park Service will know

where to look for you, should you not return. There are
many reasons for checking at the ranger station before ven-
turing off the trail. You will need current information
about snow levels, reports of grizzly bear, fire danger and
avalanche danger. If you did not write in advance for a
camping permit, you will need to get that, too.

Boating

A boat is needed to reach 2 campsites on Leigh Lake and
11 on Jackson Lake. One of the campsites on Jackson Lake
can be reached by trail, but does not offer much good
hiking. Power boats are allowed on Jackson and Jenny
lakes. There are boat-launching facilities at Colter Bay and
Signal Mountain on Jackson Lake, and also on Jenny Lake.

Only boats without motors are permitted on Leigh and
String lakes. There is a 0.25 mi. portage from String Lake
to Leigh Lake. If you have a canoe or kayak, there are
campsites on Leigh Lake that are pleasant places to spend
a night, but they don't offer easy access to any trails.

A free permit is required for all boats used in Grand
Teton National Park. Boat permits are issued at Park Headquarters in Moose.

Rafts and canoes are allowed on the Snake River with
park boat permits. It is essential to have a good background in river running. There are several rapids, many
snags and many dead-end channels on the river, which make
for an exciting trip.

You may wish to run the river with licensed river guides.
There are a great number of them offering a variety of trips.

Hand-powered craft are allowed on Two Ocean Lake.
There is one campsite at the east end of the lake. Unfortunately, the road goes there too, so it is crowded during the
height of the season.

Climbing

For those with technical mountain climbing experience, there is a Climber's Ranch north of Moose where for a small nightly fee you can sleep in a cabin.

Glenn Exum runs a guide service and climbing school at Jenny Lake. He offers an excellent beginners' class for $15 for a day's outing. There are also intermediate, advanced, and snow and ice classes. They will take you up the Grand Teton after the beginners' class if you do well. It is an enjoyable, worthwhile climb that will add something special to your visit to the Tetons.

If you plan to do any rock climbing you *must* register at the Jenny Lake Ranger Station.

Camping

Many people enjoy hiking and camping in Grand Teton National Park. In an effort to control the increasing signs of human impact, the Park Service may eventually require hikers to make reservations, or be forced to close some areas to overnight camping. Write in advance for camping permits and the latest information. Address your correspondence to: Chief Ranger, Grand Teton National Park, Moose, Wyoming 83012.

There are 5 large campgrounds on the valley floor which are usually full during July and August. There is a $3 per night camping fee, as well as a daily use permit of $2 for all park areas (unless you have the Golden Eagle or Parklands Passport).

The campground at Jenny Lake is the most scenic, as well as the most desirable for hikers. Unfortunately, it is also the most popular and difficult to get into. Your best chance is between 8:00 A.M. and 10:00 A.M. when many campers leave.

Overnight camping is permitted in all canyons, but it is necessary to obtain a permit in advance (with the exception of Garnet Canyon which is reserved for technical climbers only). The same holds true for the backcountry lakes (with the exceptions of Lake Solitude and Laurel Lake). (See camping appendices.)

Surrounding Forests

The western half of the Tetons lies in Targhee National Forest. The boundary between the park and the forest is marked along trails only. The rules for park usage are stricter than those for the forest. On occasion, rules are not observed because people do not know that they have strayed into the park from the adjoining forest. The rules that apply to all national forests apply in Targhee. There is a 14 day camping limit in any one spot. Fire permits are required only when there is a high fire danger due to extremely dry weather. No camping permits are required. Pets are allowed on the trails.

Easy access to the Tetons is provided by Teton Creek Campground in Targhee National Forest. This campground is reached via Driggs, Idaho. There is a $1 per day camping fee unless the Golden Eagle Passport is in effect.

This is a good campground because it is far less crowded than the ones in Grand Teton National Park. It is situated at the confluence of the north and south forks of Teton Creek, which flows down from Alaska Basin.

A no-fee, unimproved campground is located at the western foot of Teton Pass on Coal Creek. There is creek water to drink, a few tables scattered around and an outhouse. This campground offers access to both the southern Tetons and the adjoining Snake River Range. It is still easy to find a place to camp here, which makes it a good alternative to park campgrounds. (For a complete list of other campgrounds in Targhee National Forest see appendices.)

With the exception of the Teton Canyon Trail, which is closed to motorized vehicles, you are likely to encounter trail bikes in the national forests. Horse parties and large numbers of domestic sheep are common. You can expect to find them grazing in just the spot you want to camp—particularly in Fox Creek, Game Creek and Moose Creek.

Teton National Forest borders Grand Teton National Park on the southeast. Prior to 1972 it also bordered the park on the north where the John D. Rockefeller Parkway now is. The regulations in Targhee National Forest apply here too.

Most of the campgrounds in Teton National Forest are across the valley from the Tetons. (See appendices for a complete list.) The only area close to the Tetons, lower Black Canyon at the eastern foot of Teton Pass, has been closed to camping.

The Tetons officially end at Teton Pass. The mountains south of the pass are called the Snake River Range and are in Teton National Forest.

Access to the Tetons is provided by the Phillips Canyon Trail and the Phillips Canyon Cutoff from the Teton Pass road.

Teton Wilderness borders Grand Teton National Park on the northeast. This area is a part of Teton National Forest. The wilderness encompasses the Pinyon Peak Highlands and runs to the south boundary of Yellowstone National Park.

There are 2 major entrances to the wilderness through Grand Teton National Park. One is the Pacific Creek entrance north of Moran; the other is the Pilgrim Creek entrance east of Colter Bay. By 1974 camping permits will be required in Teton Wilderness.

Arrowhead Pool (foreground), Jenny Lake (background), from Hanging Canyon

Trail Descriptions

By Paul Lawrence

TRAIL INDEX

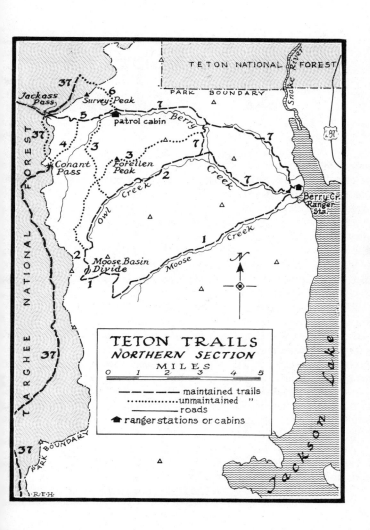

TETON TRAILS
NORTHERN SECTION
MILES
0   1   2   3   4   5

— — — maintained trails
.... unmaintained "
———— roads
⚑ ranger stations or cabins

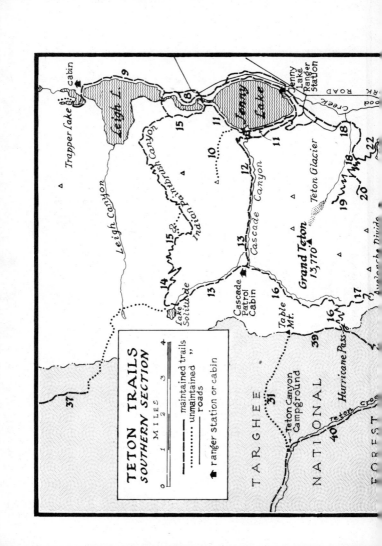

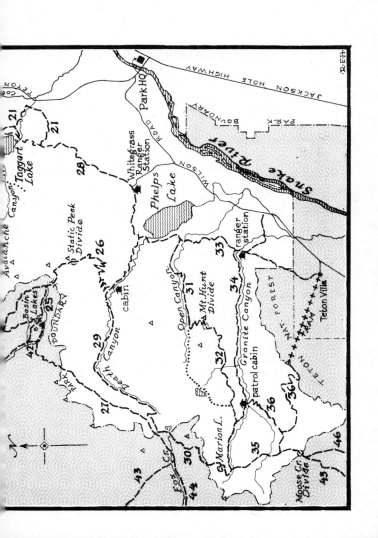

TRAIL INDEX

Con't.

Trails in the Park

NORTHERN SECTION

The northern section of Grand Teton National Park offers some excellent hiking as well as fewer hikers than elsewhere in the park. There are, however, several drawbacks to hiking in this area. Access is difficult. The trails to Webb Canyon, Owl Creek and Berry Creek are poorly maintained. Generally, this means there are no bridges, few signs and little clearing of underbrush. Detours around avalanche paths are to be expected. Even so, this area is a good place to get away from the more heavily traveled sections of the park and also for enjoying a wider variety of scenery.

Practical access to the northern section of trails in the park is by boat across Jackson Lake. The only other possibility is to hike from the reclamation road west of Flagg Ranch on a poorly marked trail which runs through numerous moose bogs and marshes.

The shortest water route to the Berry Creek Ranger Station is from the Lizard Creek Campground. This point of departure is best for hand-powered boats and small motor-driven craft. For boats requiring marine fuel or a boat ramp for launching, Colter Bay supplies all facilities.

If you are launching from Lizard Creek Campground, follow the campground loop, keeping to the right until the road parallels the lake. At this point there is an obvious

parking spot on the left (E). It is a short distance from here
to the water. Head west across the lake toward a small bay.

If you are coming from Colter Bay, go due west of the
north end of Lizard Creek Campground. On the right (N)
edge of a small bay you will see Berry Creek. (Do not go to
Moose Creek on the west edge of the bay.) Go upstream to
the landing spot that appears on the right (E). The ranger's
boat is usually beached here.

If you are planning a day's trip up Webb Canyon, or a
longer loop trip, and want to ford Berry Creek on the return rather than at the beginning, leave your boat on the
left (W) side of the creek (otherwise beach on the right (E)
side).

**Berry Creek Ranger Station (6,785 ft.)
to Moose Basin Divide (9,840 ft.)**

Mileage: 10.0

Condition: Lower section of trail easy to follow, no
bridges at creek crossings, upper section difficult to follow in spots, moderate hike.

Time: 6 to 8 hrs.

The most interesting trail in the north end of the park is the
Webb Canyon or Moose Creek Trail to the Moose Basin
divide. If you beach your boat on the left (W) side of Berry
Creek head 0.25 mi. northwest to a moraine located between Webb Canyon and Berry Creek. Climb the moraine,
and go west across a sagebrush flat until you come to the
Webb Canyon Trail.

Or, if you wish, you can simply follow the left (W) bank
of Berry Creek to Webb Canyon Trail and go from there.

This route is a bit longer.

If you beach on the right (E) side of the creek, follow the trail to the fork at Berry Creek Ranger Station. Bear left (W) and follow Berry Creek toward the mouth of a steep canyon.

After 0.25 mi. there is another junction. The left (S) fork fords Berry Creek and goes to Webb Canyon. The right (N) fork goes upstream to Owl Creek.

In the spring and early summer the fording of Berry Creek and Moose Creek can be hazardous because of the tremendous amount of runoff from melting snow. If the creek crossings look hazardous, turn back. There are other trails in the park, including a way to upper Berry Creek, which require no crossings. (See "Berry Creek Patrol Cabin to Berry Creek Ranger Station.")

In crossing deep creeks, it is not advisable to go barefoot for 2 reasons. The water is ice cold and the rocks are sharp and slippery. There are several alternatives. Some people carry very light rubber-soled canvas shoes; others carry waterproof nylon mukluks. If you don't have either one, take your socks off, put your boots back on, cross the creek, empty your boots, dry your feet and put your socks back on. It pays to carry an extra pair of socks if you plan much hiking in areas where there are no bridges.

After Berry Creek, the trail crosses a moraine toward the mouth of Webb Canyon. Although this trail is not well maintained, there are only a few downed trees blocking passage and it is quite easy to follow.

The last sign of recent maintenance is just beyond the mouth of the canyon where there is a new log bridge spanning a small spring. Do not let it build false hopes for the creek crossings ahead. At this point there is a man-made trough containing fresh spring water.

The trail continues on the north side of Moose Creek for several miles. Moose Creek drains a very large basin, Moose Basin, which accounts for the amount of water flowing into it. The trail passes steep cascades and narrow gorges. At some points it picks its way through talus slopes which reach the creek from both sides of the canyon. At times in the first 5 mi. the canyon becomes very broad, offering a wide variety of scenery. In the late summer, berry picking is usually quite good.

The first crossing of Moose Creek is 5 mi. from the patrol cabin where a huge dead tree spans the creek. The next crossing, 1 mi. farther, must be waded. If it appears to be hazardous, turn back. If you beached your boat on the west side of Berry Creek this is your last crossing before Moose Basin and the divide.

Shortly after returning to the north side of the creek, the first of a series of spectacular waterfalls appears midway up the canyon's north slope. The trail starts to climb, leaving the main creek behind. Soon it passes a second waterfall, and then a third.

As you continue up the drainage watch for a trail marker on the ridge to the right. Be sure to stay on the trail for a few hundred feet till you have passed below this post. The trail now switches back up the ridge. At this point the correct trail is visible in the distance. (It will appear that the main trail continues up the drainage toward the head of Moose Basin. This is due to heavy use by game and horsemen.)

The Ranger Peak 7½-min. quad would be very useful here. To the northeast and slightly lower in elevation you can see the Moose Basin Patrol Cabin. The small red building is in a clearing just above the creek which forms the second waterfall that you passed on the way up. The trail is a few hundred yards west of the cabin. If you cannot find it, cross the small creek on the way to the cabin, and head upstream to the first drainage entering from the north. The trail runs up this drainage on the right (E) side for over 0.25 mi., so you will be able to pick it up here.

The only other possible area of confusion occurs as the trail leaves the drainage on the right (E). After crossing several meadows, look for rock cairns or wooden posts on the slopes above and to the right (E). Head straight toward them, ascending a small ridge. The trail follows this ridge until it reaches a relatively flat plateau.

The last place you can be sure to find water in late season is the creek near the patrol cabin. Until late August there is usually some snow-melt water to be found on this plateau. The rock in this area is limestone and very porous, absorbing much of the water.

If you plan to camp in this area, the meadows in the vicinity of the patrol cabin make an ideal spot. There are a few trees there to protect you from the wind. The more hardy might wish to push on to the plateau, which is the last campsite until well into Owl Creek.

The trail again follows a slight drainage in the plateau for 0.75 mi. before switching back to the right (N). From here there is a good view of the breadth of Moose Basin and the Grand Teton appearing over the pass to the south. To the north, the Pitchstone Plateau area of Yellowstone is visible.

It is possible to keep going up the drainage to the saddle between Peak 10,422 on the right (N) and Peak 10,360 on the left (S) for a view into Idaho and the Bitch Creek drainage. This route requires a steep scramble to descend

the Bitch Creek drainage. The better route is across an un-
named pass 0.5 mi. south of Moose Mountain. You can
reach this pass by following the creek by the patrol cabin,
staying on the left (S) at all forks. (The source of this creek
lies just below the pass.) Keep Moose Mountain to your
right (N). A Forest Service trail leads from this pass to the
Bitch Creek-Camp Lake Trail on the west. (See "Connecting Trails in Targhee National Forest" for more details on
the Bitch Creek drainage.)

**Moose Basin Divide (9,840 ft.) to Junction of
Owl Creek-Berry Creek Trails (7,220 ft.)**

Mileage: 7.0

Condition: Poorly maintained, part bushwhack, moderate hike.

Time: 5 to 6 hrs.

(and routes to Forellen Peak and Upper Berry Creek)

From the top of Moose Basin divide, follow the rock cairns
where visible, or keep to the right (E) side of the divide
where the trail goes down through a notch in the limestone
wall. The 1966 Forest Service map of Teton National Forest (½ in. = 1 mi.) shows a trail branching left at this point to
the Forellen Peak divide. I could not find the trail on this
end, but it is visible from the Forellen Peak divide. The best
way to find it is to contour around—just below the limestone wall—at approximately 9,600 ft. (240 ft. lower than
the Moose Basin divide). You are now heading toward Red
Mountain, and will pass a few 100 ft. above a small lake
which is the source of Owl Creek. Pass a small creek (which

also feeds Owl Creek), and head toward the opposite ridge top. Remaining at the same elevation will bring you out on top of the ridge, at which point the trail is visible to a keen eye. As you continue down toward Owl Creek the trail is usually obvious. Where it is not, there are rock cairns which mark the way. For about 1 mi. the trail crosses open meadows, staying between 2 small streams and eventually crossing the left (W) one.

Depending on the amount of water in these drainages, this area can offer a number of campsites. By late August they may be dry.

The trail drops steadily and heads east following the now combined streams, and then switchbacks west toward the major Owl Creek drainage. Red Mountain looms to the northwest as the trail crosses the head of Owl Creek. It follows the west side of the creek for several miles, then enters a thickly wooded area in which several avalanches have occurred in the past few years. Some of these are an eighth of a mile wide. The fallen trees have not been cleared where they block the trail, necessitating troublesome detours. Generally, you can find a game trail that picks a route through the avalanche debris. It is fairly easy to find the trail again, as it stays close to the west side of Owl Creek. For a very brief stretch it crosses to the east side. Depending on the amount of water in the creek, you may want to stay on the west side to avoid wet feet.

As the trail approaches the base of Forellen Peak (9,776 ft.) it crosses a large stream flowing from the north. This is a good spot to get a drink if you plan to hike to Berry Creek via the Forellen Peak saddle because there is little water until the other side.

Years ago the Forest Service had a fire lookout on top of

Forellen Peak, and many access trails have been left as fire-control trails. These are marked by small squares of fluorescent red metal nailed to trees.

One such trail leads from Owl Creek to the Forellen Peak divide (8,900 ft.). The best way to find it is to continue past the stream, crossing to the first large meadow which is opposite the gully between Elk Mountain and Owl Peak. Head north up the open slope, staying on the right (E) of the small drainage on the west face of the slope. About half way up you will come to the trail. At this point you are 600 ft. above Owl Creek. From here the trail is easy to follow until near the divide.

If you lose the trail, head straight for the lowest point visible to the west of the Forellen Peak summit. Just below this divide you will come to the trail from Moose Basin divide which goes to the summit. At the divide you cross another trail to the summit coming from Conant Pass. Once atop the divide, a maintained park trail leads down to Berry Creek. (See "Forellen Peak Divide to Berry Creek.")

The Owl Creek Trail levels off and crosses Owl Creek south of Forellen Peak, entering an area of beaver ponds and moose bogs. The fishing is excellent and there are many good campsites. Where the trail again crosses the creek, an old Forest Service trail goes to a point just before the confluence of Berry and Owl creeks. These fordings can be avoided by hiking to Berry Creek via the Forellen Peak divide. Elk Ridge can be seen to the east as you head to the Berry Creek Trail.

> **Forellen Peak Divide (8,900 ft.)**
> **to Berry Creek Patrol Cabin (7,558 ft.)**
>
> Mileage: 2.5
>
> Condition: Not officially maintained, easy hike.
>
> Time: 1 to 2 hrs.
>
> (and routes to summit of Forellen Peak (9,776 ft.))

From the Forellen Peak divide, the trail gradually descends to Berry Creek through open meadows. Conant Pass is visible to the west and Survey Peak to the north. After 0.75 mi. the descent quickens in a series of switchbacks. If you wish to reach Conant Pass cross the creek and go west till you come to the Conant Pass Trail.

The trail continues toward the Berry Creek Patrol Cabin, passing through lower meadows which have some good campsites. The trail drops into open flats just before reaching the cabin.

When the cabin is visible, take the path to the right (N). It leads to a new bridge spanning Berry Creek. This bridge is not supposed to be here, but I won't tell if you won't.

There is an old Forest Service trail from the Forellen Peak divide passing over the summit of Forellen Peak and dropping into lower Berry Creek. This trail is easy to follow from the divide up the west ridge 0.75 mi. to the summit. There is a good view of upper Owl Creek from here, as well as Elk Mountain and Owl Peak. The trail then heads down the east ridge 3.5 mi. to Berry Creek. This trail is more difficult to follow and is recommended for the more adventurous hiker.

**Berry Creek Patrol Cabin (7,558 ft.)
to Conant Pass (8,760 ft.)**

Mileage: 2.5

Condition: Old Forest Service trail, not maintained, easy hike.

Time: 2 to 3 hrs.

This is one of the original routes into Jackson Hole. From the north side of Berry Creek opposite the patrol cabin, head across the meadows to the trail you can see ascending at the west end. Stay on the left (S) when you get to the fork, paralleling Berry Creek through open meadows. The trail climbs the north slope of the creek to Conant Pass.

On reaching the pass, a trail forks right (N) to Jackass Pass, making possible a loop return to Berry Creek Patrol Cabin. This trail follows the relatively flat ridge top north, winding in and out of Grand Teton National Park, Targhee National Forest and Idaho. (See "Connecting Trails in Targhee National Forest" for details.) There are good campsites everywhere along the ridge top.

**Berry Creek Patrol Cabin (7,558 ft.)
to Jackass Pass (8,450 ft.)**

Mileage: 1.75

Condition: Maintained, easy hike.

Time: 1 to 2 hrs.

This trail is visible at the west end of the meadow from the north side of Berry Creek (opposite the patrol cabin). Cross the meadow and follow the trail, keeping right (N) at the fork.

The trail climbs up a ridge and west to Jackass Pass. (On the flat top of the ridge, trails from Conant Pass to the south and Survey Peak to the north join the Jackass Pass Trail.) It goes into Targhee National Forest and Idaho, following an abandoned mine road. (See "Connecting Trails in Targhee National Forest" for details.) It is possible to loop either way from Jackass Pass and return to the Berry Creek Patrol Cabin.

**Berry Creek Patrol Cabin (7,558 ft.)
to Survey Peak (9,277 ft.)**

Mileage: 2.0

Condition: Not maintained, easy-moderate hike.

Time: 2 to 3 hrs.

Follow the Berry Creek Trail east from the patrol cabin 0.25 mi. to a junction with the Survey Peak Trail. This trail goes left (N) up a steep drainage, climbing to a bench east of Survey Peak. The climb is made in one long switchback. Once the bench is reached there are many excellent campsites.

The trail passes 2 small ponds. Just after the second, the trail to the summit of Survey Peak, which was once the site of a Forest Service fire lookout, forks left (S), while the main trail continues into Targhee National Forest and Idaho. (See "Connecting Trails in Targhee National Forest" for details.) The summit trail follows the northeast slopes of the peak. After 0.5 mi., the trail from Jackass Pass joins it from the right (NW). The last 0.25 mi. to the summit is steep and may require some scrambling.

Berry Creek Patrol Cabin (7,558 ft.)
to Berry Creek Ranger Station (6,785 ft.)

Mileage: 7.8 via north side of Elk Ridge, 8.2 via Owl
    Creek

Condition: Maintained, easy hike.

Time: 3 to 4 hrs.

          (and route to Hechtman Lake)

This trail is frequently used by horses. It has several obvious
unauthorized campsites. The terrain is similar to lower Owl
Creek, with open flat meadows, ponds, moose bogs and
thick willows. Berry Creek meanders through it. This route
is better for rapid travel than scenic wonder. The old mine,
visible on the north side of the canyon, is an abandoned
asbestos mine.

An old trail branches left (N) 2 mi. below the Berry
Creek Patrol Cabin and goes to Hechtman Lake (1 mi.). The
Hechtman Lake Trail leaves the Berry Creek Trail an eighth
of a mile after the Hechtman Creek crossing. This trail is
often hard to follow. It is hardly worth the effort it takes
to get to the lake. Go due north for 0.5 mi. until you reach
a large flat bench. At this point Teton National Forest
boundary signs are visible. Turn left (W) and follow the
boundary signs for almost 0.5 mi. until you cross a small
stream. Turn right (N) and follow this stream to Hechtman
Lake.

Past the Hechtman Lake Trail (0.25 mi. on the Berry
Creek Trail) you will reach Campsite 1. It is on the north-

east side of a large stream which crosses the trail. There is good fishing here. (Do not mistake the undesignated camp-site on the southeast side of Hechtman Creek for Campsite 1.) Campsite 1A is near the patrol cabin.

As the canyon narrows, the trail climbs a bit and then drops into another drainage. Here the trail forks. The right fork returns to Berry Creek and fords it, passing on the west end of Elk Ridge where it is joined by the Owl Creek Trail. Cross Berry Creek. After 0.25 mi. you will come to the old Forest Service trail from Forellen Peak. After going into the lower canyon the trail fords Berry Creek for the last time. There is good fishing here.

Owl Creek flows into Berry Creek and into a narrow canyon. The trail follows the north side of the creek closely. On the other end of this canyon lie Jackson Lake and the Berry Creek Ranger Station. At the mouth of the canyon you pass the Webb Canyon junction. Continue 0.25 mi. to the ranger station.

The left (N) fork goes to the north edge of Elk Ridge, joining a small creek which flows between Elk Ridge and Harem Hill, and eventually emptying into Jackson Lake. The left fork is a more direct route to the Berry Creek Ranger Station and avoids the crossing and recrossing of Berry Creek. It passes through several open meadows before crossing a small stream to the base of Harem Hill. Here it is joined by the trail from Flagg Ranch.

Try to enjoy the discrepancies between the old Forest Service signs, old national park signs and new national park signs. This trail is called the Conant Pass Trail, the Jackass Pass Trail or the Berry Creek Trail. It crossed the north end of Jackson Lake until the dam was built in 1916. Now a boat is the best way to complete the journey. From the south shoulder of Harem Hill the trail drops toward Jackson Lake. After recrossing the small stream it follows the shore to Berry Creek Ranger Station.

SOUTHERN SECTION

String Lake Parking Area (6,875 ft.)
to Leigh Lake (6,877 ft.)

Mileage: 0.9

Condition: Well maintained, easy hike.

Time: ½ hr.

String Lake connects Leigh Lake and Jenny Lake. On the east side of the lake is a picnic ground and a parking area. The latter is the starting point for the trail to Leigh Lake. It follows the east shore of String Lake to a bridge. Stay on the east side of the outlet following any of several trails to reach Leigh Lake.

It is possible to return to the String Lake parking area by looping up to the Paintbrush Divide Trail and following the west shore of String Lake 2.25 mi. to the outlet bridge. Cross the bridge at the outlet of Leigh Lake and follow the marked trail straight ahead. The trail to the right (N) is not maintained. It follows the west shore of Leigh Lake to the mouth of Leigh Canyon. It is still possible to follow this trail, but it is quite wet where the Paintbrush Canyon drainage enters Leigh Lake.

Continuing west from the outlet of Leigh Lake, follow the marked trail as it climbs the eastern slope of Rockchuck

Peak. It joins the Paintbrush Divide Trail 0.5 mi. from the bridge. Follow this trail left (S) to String Lake. It is a more scenic trail than the one on the east shore of String Lake and less traveled as well. Crossing open areas caused by avalanches, it passes below Laurel Lake (see "String Lake Parking Area to Lake of the Crags (Hanging Canyon)" for description), around String Lake, and joins the Jenny Lake Trail.

Leigh Lake Outlet (6,877 ft.)
to Bearpaw Lake (6,848 ft.)

Mileage: 2.8

Condition: Well maintained, easy walk.

Time: 1½ to 2 hrs.

One of the most popular short hikes in Grand Teton National Park is the Leigh Lake Trail. The lake is 2 mi. long and approximately 250 ft. deep. It drains 2 large canyons, Leigh Canyon and Paintbrush Canyon, both to the west. Mt. Moran towers over the northwest shore, sending glacial waters into the lake, giving it a greenish color.

At the outlet on the south end of Leigh Lake there is a trail from String Lake Trail to Bearpaw Lake (2.8 mi.). Take the trail closest to the shore to avoid confusion with several abandoned trails. The lake is a favorite spot for picnics and swimmers who do not mind the cool water.

The island opposite the outlet is Boulder Island. There is a good view from the enormous boulder there. It is an easy scramble to the top. You will need a boat to get there unless you swim to it, as some do. There is a sandy beach on the east side of the lake 1.3 mi. from the outlet. Near this beach is Campsite 12. This spot is a little too close to the trail to offer much privacy. The other 2 campsites on the lake are more secluded, but you need a boat to get there. Campsite 14 is at the far west shore of the lake, at the Leigh Creek inlet. Campsite 13 is on the near west shore, 0.5 mi. past the outlet.

The trail goes around the north end of the lake to the Leigh Lake Patrol Cabin. The large island at this end is Mystic Isle. Osprey nest in dead trees on the south shore.

At the patrol cabin an old, abandoned trail continues around the lake to the mouth of Leigh Canyon. The main trail goes 0.5 mi. farther north to Bearpaw Lake. It is usually less crowded than Leigh Lake.

If you go an additional 0.5 mi. to Trapper Lake, you are likely to find some solitude. You may see an occasional moose. The park maps do not show this trail, but it is easy to follow. Just continue around the north shore of Bearpaw Lake following the well-beaten path.

An old, abandoned trail continues from Trapper Lake to Moran Bay on Jackson Lake. It has become overgrown and is difficult to follow.

Water Route from String Lake to Jackson Lake
(Hand-propelled boats only)

Mileage: 4.0, 2 portages
Time: 1½ days

This route is best in early season when the water level is high. Launch your boat at the String Lake turnaround. Watch for rocks at the narrows just north of the launching site and again just above the sandbar that is midway up String Lake.

The standard portage to Leigh Lake begins just below the bridge spanning the outlet of Leigh Lake. A sign indicates the spot. This portage can be shortened by staying to the left (W) as the trail splits. This route is shorter but requires letting your boat down a steep bank to the lake. But the best way, possible only in early season, is to work around the rocks to the obvious landing on the west shore below the bridge.

Once on Leigh Lake, head for the far north end. Aim for the beach on the northwest shore of the bay. The Leigh Lake Patrol Cabin is visible from here.

Portage your boat 0.25 mi. across the sagebrush flat, crossing the Leigh Lake Trail. Do not follow the trail; head toward the southeast shore of Bearpaw Lake. Follow the outlet to the lower lake. From here it is 0.5 mi. to Jackson Lake via the outlet creek.

String Lake Parking Area (6,875 ft.)
to Lake of the Crags (9,565 ft.)
(Hanging Canyon)

Mileage: 2.25

Condition: Beaten path, not an official trail, strenuous hike due to 2,690 ft. gain in elevation.

Time: Plan all day for round trip.

There are 2 approaches to Hanging Canyon. One is from Laurel Lake, the other from the Jenny Lake Trail. In either case, park at the String Lake parking area and cross the bridge over the outlet of String Lake. Continue to the junction of the Jenny Lake-String Lake trails.

If you are going via Laurel Lake, continue west on the

String Lake Trail (right fork) until it turns north and breaks out of the trees. Take the unmarked path going up the open slopes to the left (W). This takes you to the pretty Laurel Lake which is at the bottom of the drainage between Mt. St. John on the south and Rockchuck Peak on the north. There is no camping permitted here. Follow the path to the outlet of the lake, then cross the stream and take a game trail up a steep ridge on the southwest side of the lake. This trail will take you to a boulder field. From this point, head south, traversing this field and an adjoining talus slope into the Hanging Canyon drainage. Cross the drainage to the obvious path going up the slope. Here you are approximately one-third of the way up the Hanging Canyon drainage.

A more direct but steeper route is the Jenny Lake Trail (left fork at the String Lake-Jenny Lake Trail junction) around the northwest shore of Jenny Lake to a clear but unmarked path that heads off to the right (W). This path leaves the Jenny Lake Trail approximately 0.5 mi. from the inlet of the lake. It climbs to the lip of Hanging Canyon and Arrowhead Pool. Symmetry Spire looms above to the south.

The path continues up the right (N) side of the stream to Ramshead Lake, where there are several good campsites if you wish to spend a night in the canyon. The trees here are charred from an old lightning fire.

Following the north shore of Ramshead Lake and up the talus on the west end, brings you to the largest of the 3 lakes in Hanging Canyon—Lake of the Crags. It is a truly spectacular spot. Rock of Ages is across the lake, rising almost vertically from the shore. The Jaw lies at the head of the cirque to the west, and Mt. St. John rises from the north shore. There is room for 2 people to camp by the fir trees on the north shore. Be careful crossing the snowfields surrounding the lake to avoid a cold bath.

Jenny Lake Trail (6,783 ft.)

Mileage: 6.6

Condition: Well maintained, easy hike.

Time: 3 to 4 hrs.

Jenny Lake is the focal point of visitor interest in Grand Teton National Park. Many people take the boat trip across the lake and hike the 0.5 mi. to Hidden Falls. Round trip boat fare is $1.50; one-way is 75¢. Others take scenic cruises which run hourly, or rent motor boats and explore the lake themselves. In midseason the parking area and trails are full.

Jenny Lake is 2.5 mi. long, 1.5 mi. wide and over 250 ft. deep. Located at the mouth of Cascade Canyon—with Mt. Teewinot (the Shoshone word for "many pinnacles"), the Grand Teton and Mt. Owen towering above it—the lake is one of the more spectacular scenes in the Tetons. The shore, surrounded by coniferous forest, offers the casual hiker some excellent scenery.

There is a trail which goes 6.6 mi. around Jenny Lake. At the parking area across from Jenny Lake Museum you can go either north or south along the shore. (For the shortest route to Hidden Falls and Inspiration Point see "Jenny Lake to Lake Solitude.")

If you head north, the trail goes to a bridge at the south end of String Lake and after crossing it returns to the northwest shore of Jenny Lake.

If you head south, the trail goes around the southern end of the lake. There is a bridge across Cottonwood Creek at the boat dock.

A short spur goes to the Moose Ponds from the southwest side of the lake. It comes out at the Lupine Meadows parking area and is used extensively by horse parties. Located at the foot of Mt. Teewinot, the Moose Ponds are supposed to be frequently visited by moose. I have never seen any there, but perhaps in early morning or late afternoon you might have better luck.

From the junction to the Moose Ponds, the trail passes an overlook and goes north to the boat dock. Just past the overlook is a junction with a horse trail coming from Hidden Falls. Do not go up this trail because traffic is one-way in the opposite direction. For variety, you may wish to hike back from Hidden Falls on this trail.

The trail continues around the lake to Cascade Creek. Here it forks, the left fork going to Hidden Falls and Inspiration Point, the right fork crossing the creek. Since most people take the boat across the lake to avoid the 2 mi. hike, the section of trail from the boat dock to Hidden Falls is often crowded.

If you wish to continue around the lake, cross the boat dock spur and head toward Hanging Canyon. A new horse bypass leaves the lake trail 0.25 mi. past the boat dock trail and runs to the Cascade Canyon Trail just below the Symmetry Spire couloir. The lake trail then crosses the stream rushing down from Hanging Canyon (bridge). Not far beyond is an unmarked path to the left (W) which goes up into the canyon. This is not a maintained trail. (See "String Lake Parking Area to Lake of the Crags (Hanging Canyon)" for more details.)

The lake trail goes to the outlet of String Lake and follows this stream to the bridge at the parking area. Here you head south and return to the east side of Jenny Lake.

As the trail nears the Jenny Lake parking area, there are several glacial boulders which are used by rock climbers for practice. You might have fun trying your skill on them.

Jenny Lake West Shore Boat Dock (6,783 ft.)
to Hidden Falls (6,960 ft.)
and Inspiration Point (7,200 ft.)

Mileage: 0.5 to Hidden Falls, 1.0 to Inspiration Point

Condition: Well maintained, few switchbacks, easy hike.

Time: ½ hr. to Hidden Falls, 1 hr. to Inspiration Point.

Trails run up both sides of Cascade Creek to Hidden Falls. The trail from the boat dock is on the north side of the creek. There are a total of 3 bridges across Cascade Creek, so you can choose from a number of routes. Just before reaching the falls, the horse path from the Moose Ponds Overlook joins the trail. There are hitching racks here for the horses. The best view of Hidden Falls is near the "practice rocks" of the climbing school. There is a path below the falls on the south side of the creek.

If you plan to go as far as Hidden Falls, you might as well go another 0.5 mi. to Inspiration Point for the view of the lake and valley below, and the canyon above. The trail is much steeper above Hidden Falls and has few switchbacks. Just past Inspiration Point are several unmarked paths to the left (S) which run to viewpoints above Hidden Falls.

Jenny Lake (6,783 ft.)
to Lake Solitude (9,035 ft.)

Mileage: 9.2

Condition: Well maintained, moderate hike.

Time: 4 to 6 hrs.

This is one of the most popular hikes in the park. From the Jenny Lake parking area you can ride the boat one way across the lake for 75¢, or walk around the lake 2 mi. on a well-marked trail. (See "Jenny Lake Trail.") I compromise by driving part of the way around, avoiding about 1 mi. of hiking.

Take the Lupine Meadows road just south of the Jenny Lake turn-off. It goes past the summer housing for park employees, and then crosses Cottonwood Creek and an open meadow. Just before the road turns south to Lupine Meadows, take the dirt track to the right to a small turn-around.

Park here and follow the path to the Jenny Lake Trail, past the Moose Ponds to the west shore boat dock. From here, there is a well-marked trail 0.5 mi. to Hidden Falls, then on to Inspiration Point. I hurry along this stretch because the Hidden Falls area tends to resemble Grand Central Station during the rush hour.

Beyond Inspiration Point there are fewer people. A new horse bypass returns to Jenny Lake from just below the Symmetry Spire couloir, which rises to the north. Many climbers have worn a path to the couloir. It leaves the trail 100 yds. beyond the horse bypass. **WARNING**: Do not attempt to ascend this couloir alone, without a rope, or without an ice axe. Check at Jenny Lake Ranger Station.

The trail continues up the canyon with good views of Mt. Teewinot, Mt. Owen and the Grand Teton. Where the trail crosses talus slopes there are many wild raspberries and thimbleberries in late August. Despite the heavy use of this trail, most people do not stop to pick them, leaving all the more for me.

Shortly before reaching the forks of the canyon, the trail crosses a wide stream. This is a good spot for lunch. If you look across Cascade Creek you will see a stream rushing down from Valhalla Canyon, a hanging canyon that is a spectacular place to visit, and a good place to camp. There is no trail. To reach it you must wade the creek and bush-whack up the right (W) side of the stream for approximately 2,000 ft. Check at Jenny Lake Ranger Station.

If you are not accustomed to mountain water (the human and horse traffic up Cascade Canyon grows every year), bring your own water or drink from the several springs along the way. I drink from Cascade Creek.

There are 2 designated campsites along this trail. The first, Campsite 18, is less than 1 mi. below the Cascade Forks. At the fork's, bear right to Lake Solitude. Campsite 17 is just beyond the Cascade Ranger Station.

Before too long the trail breaks out above the timberline where you will have a good view of the Grand Teton, Mt. Owen and Mt. Teewinot down the canyon. In the talus slopes below Lake Solitude the squeaks of pikas can be heard, and an occasional marmot sighted.

The trail climbs the moraine to the lake and follows the east shore. There is good drinking water from springs on the north side of the lake and there is a fiberglass outhouse. The view is better from the north. No camping is allowed here.

Lake Solitude (9,035 ft.)
to Paintbrush Divide (10,720 ft.)

Mileage: 2.4

Condition: Trail often snow covered, difficult hike.

Time: 2 to 3 hrs.

   (and route from Lake Solitude to Leigh Canyon)

From Lake Solitude one can climb to Paintbrush divide via the trail, or bushwhack up over a saddle into Leigh Canyon. The easiest way to accomplish this is to angle up to the lowest point from the north shore of the lake. (Avoid the steeper eastern slope.) When you have gained sufficient elevation to put you above the steep ledges, traverse east to the saddle. **WARNING**: Do not attempt this climb in early or midseason without an ice axe. In the fall it is just a scramble; with snow and ice it could be dangerous.

   From the saddle, descend into a hanging canyon, keeping left (N) until you reach open meadows. Follow the stream which flows into Leigh Canyon just below Mink Lake. Here there is a good campsite. Be sure to check at the Jenny Lake Ranger Station before you leave if you plan to descend into Leigh Canyon.

   To reach Paintbrush divide, stay on the trail to the northeast shore of Lake Solitude. Take the right (E) fork up the canyon wall. The trail quickly becomes steep as it climbs to a ridge overlooking a hanging canyon. With caution, it is possible to descend into this canyon if there is no snow. However, the recommended route is the one previously described. Check at the Jenny Lake Ranger Station for off-trail conditions.

The air gets thin up here, so keep a slow but steady pace. Paintbrush divide is snow covered until late August and again by mid-October. To the east of the divide are the Gros Ventre and Wind River ranges. Grizzly Bear Lake in Leigh Canyon can be seen to the left (N), as well as Jackson Lake down Paintbrush Canyon.

Paintbrush Divide (10,720 ft.)
to String Lake Parking Area (6,875 ft.)

Mileage: 7.9

Condition: Trail difficult to find just over the divide, then generally well maintained, easy hiking except for the descent from the divide.

Time: 3 to 5 hrs.

The old trail drops due east off the divide and switchbacks down to the Leigh Canyon divide. Since it is often covered with a snow cornice, a new trail has been built to the north. At the top of the divide the trail goes to the left (N) and climbs up the ridge of the adjoining peak for several hundred feet before switching down. This trail is often in need of repair and is not always clearly marked. You must be careful on this rocky moraine because there are loose rocks over the trail.

An alternative is to glissade down the snow-covered divide to the Leigh Canyon divide. **WARNING**: This should be attempted only by people who know how to use an ice axe.

A third possibility is to use an ice axe as a support and work your way down between the rock slopes on the north and the steep snow on the divide. You should have little trouble if you are careful.

When you reach the Leigh Canyon divide, the trail is again clearly visible and easy to follow as it heads down Paintbrush Canyon to the right (SE).

At this point you may want to take a side trip to Grizzly Bear Lake on the side of Leigh Canyon. There is an unmarked trail on the divide that goes toward the lake. (It is not suggested to hike down to Leigh Lake. There is no trail through the dense willows and you will have to ford the creek a number of times. It is best to return to Paintbrush Canyon after visiting Grizzly Bear Lake, having left your packs at the divide.)

An unmarked foot trail runs from below the divide to Holly Lake, forking left. This is shorter than the conventional trail.

The main trail works down to the Holly Lake junction. You can see Holly Lake beside Mt. Woodring from just below the Leigh Canyon divide. It is easily reached by a short side trail that is clearly marked. Here again, if you have the time, leave your packs at the junction and walk to the lake. It is a pleasant place for lunch.

The trail drops rapidly from the Holly Lake junction into the canyon. The water here is good. The trail enters a dense coniferous forest above Leigh Lake, which you can glimpse through the trees below

At the String Lake-Leigh Lake junction, take the right (S) fork to the String Lake parking area. It is shorter and more scenic. If you have never seen Leigh Lake, take the left (N) fork which goes to the lake and then turns back to the String Lake parking area. Watch for moose.

If you have only one vehicle, it is easy to hitch a ride

back to Jenny Lake from the junction of the String Lake and Jenny Lake roads.

In the past, the hike from Jenny Lake to String Lake via Lake Solitude and Paintbrush divide was the favorite over-night hike in Grand Teton National Park. However, no camping has been allowed at Lake Solitude since 1972. It is still possible to make the trip and camp at Holly Lake instead. No off-trail camping permits are being issued from Campsite 17 to Paintbrush divide. Thus, the remaining al-ternatives are to stay at Campsite 17, or below the divide and at Holly Lake on the north side.

If you stay at Campsite 17, walk up to Lake Solitude in early evening to see the alpenglow on the Grand Teton reflected in the lake. It is a sight well worth the short hike. There are wildflowers, including a canyonful of Indian paintbrush in July and August.

**Forks of Cascade Canyon (7,840 ft.)
to Hurricane Pass (10,372 ft.)**

Mileage: 5.1

Condition: Well maintained, moderate hike.

Time: 2½ to 4 hrs.

(See "Jenny Lake to Lake Solitude" for trail description to this point.)

The trail above the forks is less traveled than the lower section, although both are popular. From the junction, the trail passes under a large rock wall of black schist. It then heads south toward a series of glacial stair steps. Approxi-mately 1 mi. from the forks, a long stream can be seen flowing into the south fork of Cascade Creek. (This stream can be followed up to Dartmouth Basin which is below the west face of the Grand Teton. There is no trail. Check at the Jenny Lake Ranger Station.)

From this point the trail climbs more rapidly, switching back a number of times. It reaches a good viewpoint at the top of the last switchback. To the southwest, Table Mountain is visible, and to the northeast, Mt. St. John.

After 1 mi., the trail enters a whitebark pine forest which contains the largest specimens of this tree known in the world. Campsite 19 is near here. Look for the sign which indicates its location. It is past some sites on the left (E) side of the trail. Campsite 19A, 1 mi. farther, is for horse parties only.

Soon the trail passes under the sheer, east wall of Table Mountain. There are several undesignated campsites in this area if you can get a permit. The trail heads toward the last glacially carved bench, going due east for a short stretch. The rushing stream in the distance comes from Icefloe Lake. Cascade Creek forks with the trail switching up the rim, leaving most of the trees behind. From the top of the last switchback there is a good view of Table Mountain to the northwest. On this last bench the trail is fairly level to the junction with the Avalanche Canyon Divide Trail.

Campsite 20 is east of this junction. It is less crowded than Campsite 19. If Campsite 20 is full, request a permit for the area above on the Avalanche Canyon Divide Trail, or go on to Sunset Lake. Until late in the season it is usually wet from here to the top of Hurricane Pass.

Switching back and forth up the headwall, you can see Schoolroom Glacier, named for its almost perfect form. Depending on the time of year, you can see crevasses in the glacier and the bergschrund where ice has pulled away from the headwall. Just about any time, you can see the classic terminal and lateral moraines and a small lake at the base of the glacier. The water is milky in color due to powdered rock, known as glacial flour, caused by the ice scraping the rock beneath it. The notch in the terminal moraine was created by water flowing out of this small lake. There is a good view of the limestone wall from the trail. Avalanche divide is visible between the far end of the wall and the South Teton. The last switchback takes you to the top of Hurricane Pass.

**South Fork of Cascade Canyon (9,600 ft.)
to Avalanche Canyon Divide (10,600 ft.)**

Mileage: 1.6

Condition: Poorly maintained, moderate hike.

Time: 1 hr.

(and route to Icefloe Lake)

From the trail junction near Campsite 20 (the sign is usually lying on the ground), take the left (E) fork following the old Skyline Trail. In the past it led to Alaska Basin, but has been abandoned from the Avalanche Canyon Divide because of the unstable rock on the wall.

After crossing the creek the trail heads toward the wall. There is a lot of snow here until late season. The trail switches up a ridge to the east, goes north for 0.25 mi. and then turns east again to a plateau where there are good campsites. From this plateau the view down U-shaped Cascade Canyon is excellent.

Icefloe Lake (10,652 ft.) is a short side trip. Leave the trail at the point where it turns sharply south toward Avalanche Divide. Follow this contour north, angling up the small bench more than 200 ft. above the trail and almost 0.5 mi. north. From here, cross the snowfield and talus to the lake less than 0.25 mi. away. It is just below the saddle between the South and Middle Tetons. This is an easy side trip and should take about ½ hr. round trip. Icefloe Lake is not a particularly comfortable place to camp. Go back to the shelter of the plateau or upper Avalanche Canyon for a campsite if you plan to spend the night.

Officially, the trail stops here. It is not advisable to follow the old trail any farther. However, it is an easy scramble down to Kit and Snowdrift lakes. There is a steep snowfield just over the divide until very late in the season. This should be descended with an ice axe for safety. Check conditions at Jenny Lake Ranger Station before visiting any of these off-trail lakes. Snowdrift Lake has some excellent spots for camping if high winds do not bother you. (For a route down the canyon see "Taggart Lake Parking Area to Avalanche Canyon.")

Lupine Meadows (6,740 ft.)
to Surprise Lake (9,550 ft.)
and Amphitheater Lake (9,700 ft.)

Glacier Trail

Mileage: 4.6

Condition: Well maintained, strenuous hike.

Time: 3 to 4 hrs.

Because this trail is the standard approach for parties ascending the Grand Teton, and since it offers the day hiker a chance to see some spectacular high mountain scenery, it is very often impossible to hike it without being in sight of another party much of the time. In 1972 the park closed the trail to horse travel, but overcrowding remains a problem. An early start will get you ahead of most of the hikers. It is possible to camp at Surprise or Amphitheater lakes. It is not a place to seek solitude because many climbers base camp here.

This trail is a good day hike. Because of the gain in elevation, nearly 3,000 ft. in 4.6 mi., you should not attempt it on your first day in the area. You should be fully acclimated to the altitude and in good shape before starting up the many switchbacks of this trail.

To reach the Lupine Meadows parking area, take the dirt road which goes west from the highway just south of the Jenny Lake turn-off. Bear right over Cottonwood Creek, then due west until the road swings south to Lupine Meadows.

If you wish to go from Surprise Lake to Garnet Canyon, follow the drainage from the lake down a steep gully. The drainage runs out of the south side of the lake and eventually crosses the Garnet Canyon Trail. From here you can go farther into the canyon or return to the Lupine Meadows parking area. Check at the Jenny Lake Ranger Station if you plan this variation in routes. There is no established trail from Surprise Lake into Garnet Canyon.

Continuing to Amphitheater Lake from Surprise Lake is an easy walk. It is only 0.2 mi. farther and approximately 150 ft. higher. Follow the trail around the north shore of

Surprise Lake or, for a more picturesque route, follow the stream which runs into the west end of the lake. There is a small waterfall that is quite pretty.

Amphitheater Lake is at the foot of Disappointment Peak in a cirque which resembles an amphitheater. The trail swings around the north shore of the lake, passing the tents of climbers who are usually camped here. Officially, the trail ends on the saddle just north of the lake. From here you can see into Glacier Gulch. Down the gulch and to the east is Delta Lake, milky in color due to glacial flour. To the west, the large moraine of Teton Glacier is visible.

In late June and through July there are many mosquitoes in the lower sections of the trail, so put on insect repellent when you leave your car and carry some with you.

The trail follows the base of the range for 1.7 mi., crosses the milky creek (bridge) rushing down from Glacier Gulch, and runs through a lodgepole pine forest to a junction with the Bradley Lake Trail. At this point you will start to climb 19 switchbacks of varying length. There are 2 springs on the lower portion of the trail which have good drinking water.

The switchbacks go up the ridge between Glacier Gulch on the north and Garnet Canyon on the south. From here you can see Bradley and Taggart lakes. The trail to Garnet Canyon starts at the fifth switchback. It is well marked. More difficult to spot is the trail which leaves from a switchback to the right (N) and goes to Surprise Lake. You are likely to find other people there.

For a good view, climb the pinnacle southeast of the lake.

> **Amphitheater Lake (9,700 ft.)**
> **to Teton Glacier (10,080 ft.)**
> Mileage: 1.5
> Condition: Difficult route over snow until late season.
> Time: 2 hrs.

WARNING: This route can be hazardous until late summer when snow has left the north slope of Disappointment Peak. It is recommended that only those with experience on high-angle snow and equipped with an ice axe attempt this traverse. Check at Jenny Lake Ranger Station for a report on snow conditions.

Follow the trail to the saddle just north of Amphitheater Lake. From here the moraine of Teton Glacier is visible. There is a path that heads under the north wall of Disappointment Peak, dropping slightly as it goes west. It crosses some rock slopes that are slippery when they are wet.

A fixed cable hangs in a spot which has slight exposure. Follow it down to the snow, heading for the trail ahead. The snow traverse begins here under the north wall of Disappointment Peak (named by early climbers who thought they were ascending the east face of the Grand Teton). Stay as high as you can, keeping between the moraine of a small glacier and the north face of Disappointment Peak. As soon as you are level with this moraine on your right (N), cross it and descend to the ice and snow of the glacier. Aim for the east face of the Grand Teton where the Teton Glacier joins it. Ascend the moraine at this point. Look for the routes used by other parties; they are less likely to slide. Use care when others are below you to avoid starting rock slides.

At the top of the moraine you can see the glacier to the west. In the 1920's you could step off the moraine onto the glacier, but not today. To reach the surface of the glacier, traverse the snow under the east face of the Grand Teton, heading around it to the west. Watch for crevasses. *Do not* attempt to scale the glacier to Gunsight Notch. There is constant falling rock.

Garnet Canyon Spur

Mileage: 1.0

Condition: Well maintained, moderate hike.

Time: 1 hr.

To reach Garnet Canyon take the spur trail from the fifth switchback on the Amphitheater Lake Trail. It goes approximately 1 mi. up into the canyon. It officially stops in a boulder field on the canyon floor. This spot is known as The Platforms.

Garnet Canyon is one of the most popular base camp areas for climbers because of its easy access to climbing routes on the Grand Teton and other nearby peaks. This area is so heavily used by climbers that above The Platforms, no camping permits are issued to hikers. Only technical climbers may apply for permits.

Those with high-mountain experience can follow the climbers' path up the canyon toward Spalding Falls and Petzoldt Caves. Check at Jenny Lake Ranger Station first. There is a good view of Middle Teton Glacier and the black diabase dike in the Middle Teton.

Taggart Lake Parking Area (6,625 ft.)
to Taggart Lake (6,902 ft.)

Mileage: 1.6

Condition: Well maintained, easy hike.

Time: 1 hr.

This trail to the twin piedmont lakes at the mouth of Avalanche and Garnet canyons is heavily traveled, since it is a short, easy hike. From the parking area, the trail skirts the Taggart Lake moraine and heads up the north side of Taggart Creek.

The Bradley Lake Trail branches right (N) 1 mi. from the parking area. The Taggart Lake Trail continues left (W) 0.5 mi. to the south end of Taggart Lake. Camping is no longer permitted here.

Here you may continue north around the lake, climb the moraine between Taggart and Bradley lakes and drop down to the Bradley Lake Trail, or, you can go south 1.25 mi., looping back to the parking area via a section of the Valley Trail that runs to the White Grass Ranger Station and the Beaver Creek Trail (2.25 mi.).

Taggart Lake Parking Area (6,625 ft.)
to Bradley Lake (7,022 ft.)

Mileage: 2.0

Condition: Well maintained, easy hike.

Time: 1 hr.

(For a description of the trail from the parking area to the Bradley Lake Trail junction see "Taggart Lake Parking Area to Taggart Lake.")

At the junction take the right fork (N). The Bradley Lake Trail climbs the moraine between Bradley and Taggart lakes. There is a good view from here. It then switches down to Bradley Lake. At the southeast edge of the lake you will come to a trail from Taggart Lake. This is a pleasant way to return to the parking area. Because it is a bit farther from the parking area, Bradley Lake is less crowded than Taggart Lake. No camping permits are issued for either one.

The trail goes around the east shore, crossing the outlet of the lake (bridge). Past the lake it climbs the moraine on the north side. (From the top of this moraine you can look up at Bannock Falls in Garnet Canyon.) It contours around to the Glacier Trail. From Bradley Lake to the Glacier Trail is 3 mi.

Taggart Lake Parking Area (6,625 ft.)
to Forks of Avalanche Canyon (7,760 ft.)

Mileage: 4.5

Condition: Not an official trail, path difficult to follow,
       moderate hike.

Time: 2 to 3 hrs.

       (and route to Taminah and Snowdrift lakes)

(For a description of the trail to Taggart Lake see "Taggart Lake Parking Area to Taggart Lake.")

From the Taggart Lake Trail, an unmarked path continues around the north shore to Taggart Creek. To locate it, follow the Taggart Lake Trail to the moraine between Taggart and Bradley lakes. Before the first switchback there is a large dead tree lying to your left (W). The path is just below this fallen tree.

Head around the west end of Taggart Lake through some moose bogs. Wet feet are often unavoidable here. The path joins Taggart Creek by dropping down to it from the slope on the north. Stay on the right (N) side of the creek to the forks. Where the path is blocked, animals have made new paths which eventually rejoin it. The area around the forks is ideal moose habitat. Keep a sharp lookout to avoid bumping into one.

From here, Shoshoko Falls in the north fork of Taggart Creek is visible.

To continue up the canyon requires some basic mountaineering skills. Check at Jenny Lake Ranger Station. To reach Lake Taminah, stay on the north side of the north fork, passing to the right of the falls. Climb the rock slabs or scramble up the gullies until you reach a steep snowfield. Traverse the top of the snowfield south to the rim of the Taminah Lake bench. Stay on the north shore to the rocky meadow at the west end. I do not recommend camping here; it is too rocky and wet.

To reach Snowdrift Lake, head up the northwest side of the steep slopes behind Taminah Lake. Climb up the drainage, staying on the north side. Near the top, head back south toward the stream and the bench of Snowdrift Lake. On the north shore of the lake and on another bench just above it, there is good camping.

Avalanche divide is visible to the northwest. It is an easy

scramble or snow climb to the divide. (See "South Fork of Cascade Canyon to Avalanche Canyon Divide.")

Hurricane Pass (10,372 ft.)
to Basin Lakes (9,550 ft.)

Mileage: 3.0

Condition: Forest Service trail, well maintained, easy
      hike.

Time: 2 hrs.

From the top of Hurricane Pass you can look west down the Roaring Creek Fork of Teton Canyon. There is a game trail that goes down into the canyon. Since the canyon is in Targhee National Forest you need not check at Jenny Lake Ranger Station if you want to bushwhack down. It is not particularly recommended, however, because of the steep scramble in the main fork of Teton Canyon. (See "Table Mountain to Hurricane Pass" for the traverse from Hurricane Pass to Table Mountain.)

The trail climbs higher from Hurricane Pass, going above Schoolroom Glacier. Just before the top of the ridge it enters Targhee National Forest. From here the trail gradually descends into Alaska Basin. This huge basin is glacier carved and offers many fine camping sites.

Battleship Mountain is on the right (W) as the trail begins a series of switchbacks down to Sunset Lake (9,608 ft.), 1.7 mi. from Hurricane Pass. The wall and Avalanche Canyon beyond, lie to the left (E). You can get an occasional glimpse of the Grand Teton through a notch in the wall.

Sunset Lake is too crowded for me, but you may wish to

join the other campers and the porcupine family that makes its home there.

The trail forks 0.5 mi. from Sunset Lake. The left fork goes southeast toward the head of Alaska Basin, Buck Mountain and Static Peak, eventually dropping into Death Canyon. The right fork goes down to the Basin Lakes 1.5 mi. farther. There are a number of switchbacks that wind down the north slope of Alaska Basin. From there you can look across to the Sheep Steps and Mt. Meek Pass.

Just before you reach the first of the 8 small Basin Lakes, the Teton Canyon Trail enters from the right (W). (For a description of this trail see "Teton Canyon Campground to Basin Lakes.") After crossing a small stream, the trail forks. The left fork passes on the north side of the lakes and joins the trail going to Death Canyon at the head of the Basin. The right fork goes around the west side of the lakes and continues up the Sheep Steps to Death Canyon Shelf.

There are usually many campers at the Basin Lakes. With some effort you can probably find a spot all to yourself. Remember that mosquitoes come very late to the high country and flourish long after they have left the valley floor.

Upper Alaska Basin (9,575 ft.)
to Static Peak Divide (10,800 ft.)

Mileage: 3.7 from Sunset Lake (9,608 ft.), 2.3 from Basin Lakes (9,550 ft.)

Condition: Well maintained, moderate hike.

Time: 2 to 3 hrs.

From the junction 0.5 mi. past Sunset Lake, the trail gradually climbs the north slopes of Alaska Basin. There are a
few good campsites in the first mile. If you look east
toward the col below Veiled Peak, you will see the Old
Skyline Trail that runs into Alaska Basin joining this trail
between Veiled Peak and Buck Mountain. It has been abandoned. You can use it for access to upper Avalanche Canyon, but this would require an ice axe through most of the
season. Check at Jenny Lake Ranger Station.

As the trail approaches Buck Mountain, it is joined by
the 1.5 mi. long trail from Basin Lake. The park sign on the
Buck Mountain divide can be seen from here.

Early in the season it is impossible to descend from the
saddle at the divide without an ice axe. Check at Jenny
Lake Ranger Station for conditions.

Once across the divide you are in Grand Teton National
Park. The trail skirts the southwest wall of Buck Mountain,
passing a small lake to the right (S), and goes up the west
shoulder of Static Peak. Here again, snow in early season
can make the trail treacherous. This is a most impressive
area. You can look 3,000 ft. down into Death Canyon and
straight up at the massive south face of Buck Mountain.

Static Peak divide is the highest point on a maintained
trail in the Tetons (10,800 ft.). Do not push your pace at
this altitude.

This trail gives you the chance to climb Static Peak
(11,303 ft.), the highest peak south of Buck Mountain. It is
only 0.25 mi. and 500 ft. up from the divide to the summit.
From the top of the divide, simply follow the south ridge
to the summit. It is more of a walk than a climb. The view
is superb, with Buck Mountain and the Grand Teton to the
north, Jackson Hole to the east, Timberline Lake below and
Death Canyon and Prospector's Mountain to the south.

Static Peak Divide (10,800 ft.)
to Death Canyon Patrol Cabin (7,841 ft.)

Mileage: 3.0

Condition: Well maintained, dangerous when snow
    covered, easy downhill hike.

Time: 1½ to 2 hrs.

Only the most hardy should venture up this steep trail with its numerous switchbacks, especially with a pack. I do not recommend it when there is such a pleasant way to descend from Alaska Basin. The best short loop is to ascend Death Canyon and follow the Death Canyon Shelf to Mt. Meek Pass into Alaska Basin. Check on snow conditions at Jenny Lake Ranger Station. In early season it is dangerous to use this route without thorough knowledge of high-angle snow technique using an ice axe.

From the Static Peak divide the trail follows the ridge line and then drops off to a steep slope. The snow stays here for a long time. Be careful if there is much snow on the trail. One slip here and you could end up in a pile of rocks 400 ft. below. When clear of snow the trail is safe.

After coming down the steep slopes, the trail reaches a saddle where it begins a series of long switchbacks down to Death Canyon through a whitebark pine forest. Just below the saddle, you reach the Phelps Lake Overlook, with a good view of the lake and the surrounding country. The upper section of trail stays to the left (E) of the stream that rushes down from Static Peak, crossing it about halfway down, and recrossing shortly before the Death Canyon Patrol Cabin. By this time you will be tired of the numerous switchbacks, but do not shortcut.

Basin Lakes (9,550 ft.)
to Fox Creek Pass (9,600 ft.)

Mileage: 5.7

Condition: Well maintained, moderate hike.

Time: 2 to 3 hrs.

From Basin Lakes in Targhee National Forest the trail crosses Teton Creek, heading west toward a break in the limestone wall. The switchbacks leading up over the wall are known as the Sheep Steps. They were rebuilt in the summer of 1972, so it is now possible to avoid crossing the lingering snowfields below the wall. Once on top, the trail levels out to traverse the Death Canyon Shelf. The Devil's Stair Trail branches right (W) 2 mi. from Basin Lakes. (See "Teton Canyon Shelf to Teton Canyon Campground" for a description.)

Past this junction 0.25 mi. is Mt. Meek Pass (9,726 ft.), an entry into Grand Teton National Park. The relatively flat shelf offers many fine campsites. Check on permits for this area. Here there are many springs, open meadows, and a fine view down Death Canyon.

On the shelf, the trail passes to the east of Fossil Mountain and drops into Fox Creek Pass. The ruins of an old trapper cabin can be seen on the left (E).

**White Grass Ranger Station (6,780 ft.)
to Taggart Lake (6,902 ft.)**
Valley Trail
Mileage: 4.5
Condition: Well maintained, easy hike.
Time: 2 hrs.

The Valley Trail is officially 24.5 mi. long, from Teton Village to Bearpaw Lake. All sections except White Grass Ranger Station to Taggart Lake are covered in the descriptions of other trails. I do not particularly recommend hiking the entire Valley Trail; it is not very exciting.

The section from White Grass Ranger Station to Taggart Lake follows the base of Static Peak, Buck Mountain and Mt. Wister. There are several streams which cross the trail (bridges) providing water for out-of-the-way picnics.

From the White Grass Ranger Station take the right (N) fork at the trail junction. The White Grass Ranch uses portions of this trail for horse parties. There are several unauthorized side trails branching from the main one.

**White Grass Ranger Station (6,780 ft.)
to Fox Creek Pass—Death Canyon (9,600 ft.)**
Mileage: 9.2
Condition: Well maintained, moderate hike.
Time: 5 to 6 hrs.

To reach the White Grass Ranger Station, turn west off the Moose-Wilson road at the junction 3.1 miles south of Park Headquarters in Moose. Follow the White Grass Ranch road to the ranch gate. Bear left on the dirt road which passes a fence line, swings west, fords a small creek and ends at a parking area just east of the ranger station.

From here the trail climbs a moraine north of Phelps Lake 0.9 mi. to an overlook (7,202 ft.). Watch for thimbleberries in the wooded section near the ranger station in late July and early August. From the overlook, the trail switches down the moraine to the west shore of Phelps Lake (6,800 ft.). Here a spur leads to the lake shore and Campsite 28.

Boats are allowed on Phelps Lake. A small rubber raft might not be too difficult to carry in. If you wonder how the large power boats got on the lake, there is a private road where the JY Ranch is located.

The Valley Trail goes to Open Canyon from a junction on the northwest side of the lake (left fork). The Death Canyon Trail forks right (W), going between the massive walls of Death Canyon. Here it begins to switchback up the north wall. This section is steep. When snow covers these switchbacks you must be careful to avoid sliding into the creek. Trail crews attempt to clear this section early in the season because of its heavy use.

The trail reaches the flat floor of the canyon where it narrows. The rock walls here are gneiss and schist, forming an impressive portal. The canyon broadens out and the creek that was rushing and tumbling in the lower canyon, meanders quietly along forming placid pools.

At 0.75 mi. from the lip (3.7 mi. from White Grass Ranger Station), is the Death Canyon Patrol Cabin. Here the trail to Static Peak and Alaska Basin branches right (N).

(See "Static Peak Divide to Death Canyon Patrol Cabin" for a description.)

Campsite 26, a popular spot, is 0.3 mi. past the patrol cabin. From here you can look up the switchbacks of the Static Peak Trail. Where the stream from Rimrock Lake joins the main creek you cross (bridge) to the south side. Rimrock Lake is on the north shoulder of Prospector Mountain and can be seen from the Static Peak Trail. You can reach it by bushwhacking up the right (W) side of this stream and scaling the falls below the outlet. **WARNING**: This is for technical climbers only. A rope is required. Check at Jenny Lake Ranger Station.

As the Death Canyon Trail heads up the canyon it crosses another stream flowing from the south (bridge). This is the outlet of the Forget-Me-Not-Lakes which can be reached from upper Death Canyon. To the west, the Death Canyon Shelf is visible with (left to right) Mt. Bannon, Mt. Jedediah Smith and Mt. Meek rising behind it.

As the trail recrosses Death Canyon Creek, watch for the new bridge. Campsite 27 is 3.5 mi. past Campsite 26. Beyond it, the trail crosses the creek again. At this spot it is easy to miss a bridge which is several hundred yards downstream from the trail crossing.

Now the canyon swings south below Death Canyon Shelf. The trail again crosses the creek (bridge), to the head of the canyon where it turns west toward Fox Creek Pass. The ruins of an old trapper cabin are on the right (N). The last section of trail is quite steep. A snowfield which remains through much of the season lies to the east of the pass. Unfortunately, this is exactly where the trail goes. Early in the season you need an ice axe for safety. Later it is possible to scramble around the snowfield to the top of the pass. **WARNING**: Do not attempt to cross this snow-

field at any time without an ice axe. If you do not have
one, go around it. You can probably avoid the snowfield
after midseason. Check at Jenny Lake Ranger Station for
conditions.

Fox Creek Pass (9,600 ft.)
to Marion Lake (9,240 ft.)

Mileage: 2.3

Condition: Well maintained, easy hike.

Time: 1 hr.

Fox Creek Pass straddles the Grand Teton National Park-
Targhee National Forest boundary. From here you can see
into Idaho to the west.

There are several good campsites on the pass. The best
one is near Pass Lake, which is just inside the park boundary. You will need a permit to camp here. There is a good
view of Fossil Mountain to the northwest and Spearhead
Peak to the south. Both of these mountains are in Targhee
National Forest.

Just over the pass, the Fox Creek Trail joins the Skyline
or Teton Crest Trail. (See "Connecting Trails in Targhee
National Forest" and "Skyline or Teton Crest Trail" in
"Recommended Longer Hikes in Grand Teton National
Park" for details.) It skirts the west side of Spearhead Peak
and heads for a small saddle below the northeast ridge of
Housetop Mountain. From this saddle there is an impressive
view of both forks of upper Granite Canyon.

A traverse along the south slopes of Fox Creek Pass
takes you to an overlook above Indian Lake. It is also possi-

ble to continue to the Forget-Me-Not-Lakes by contouring around the south rim of Death Canyon.

The trail drops 260 ft. in the 0.5 mi. to Marion Lake from the saddle. Campsite 32 is located here.

White Grass Ranger Station (6,780 ft.)
to Mt. Hunt Divide (9,710 ft.)

Mileage: 7.3

Condition: Maintained, moderate hike.

Time: 4 to 5 hrs.

(and route to Coyote Lake)

(For a description of the trail to Phelps Lake see "White Grass Ranger Station to Fox Creek Pass.")

From the junction of the Death Canyon-Phelps Lake Trail go left (S) around the west shore of Phelps Lake for 1 mi. The Open Canyon Trail to Mt. Hunt divide branches. Head northwest, climbing the lower slope of Prospector Mountain. It is joined in 0.75 mi. by a trail from the Granite Canyon parking area.

The trail traverses the north slope of Open Canyon, into an open area well above a creek. It then follows the same contour until reaching the creek. After crossing (bridge), it stays on the south side, gradually switching back toward the head of the canyon.

Just before leaving the creek and heading south to the Mt. Hunt divide, a short path leads to Campsite 29. This picturesque campsite is very popular, so make reservations well in advance.

The trail starts to climb much more steeply. A series of switchbacks brings you to a plateau northwest of the summit of Mt. Hunt.

If you plan to travel to the head of Open Canyon and Coyote Lake, the easiest point of departure is just above the last switchback. Traverse a long talus slope, heading toward the creek. From here the going is easier. Once you are below the Open Canyon divide, you can see the outlet stream of Coyote Lake. Scramble up the stream, keeping on the west side of the lake. There are not any good campsites at the lake, so if you wish to camp, do so in the meadows below the divide. Be careful in the steep snowfields crossing the divide. Check at Jenny Lake Ranger Station.

The trail to Mt. Hunt divide continues southwest on the plateau to a final series of switchbacks which take you to the top.

Mt. Hunt Divide (9,710 ft.)
to Granite Canyon Trail (8,360 ft.)

Mileage: 4.1

Condition: Poorly maintained, hard to follow just above the Granite Canyon Trail junction, moderate hike.

Time: 2 hrs.

(and routes to Indian Lake)

Just over the Mt. Hunt divide from Open Canyon, the trail is rough, but it improves beyond the talus field. After circling south of the Mt. Hunt summit it drops into Granite Canyon. In 1.25 mi. the trail levels off and contours around the south slope of Mt. Hunt.

The first large drainage you cross is the outlet from Indian Lake. It is possible to follow this stream to the lake, but it requires some steep scrambling.

An easier route is past the second stream crossing, angling northwest up the drainage, keeping right (E). This drainage ends in a large cirque. Go around the point on the right (E) to an overlook. Then head due north across a small talus slope to the moraine south of Indian Lake. This is a strenuous hike recommended for advanced hikers only. Check at Jenny Lake Ranger Station. There are many excellent campsites at the lake.

It is possible to traverse from Indian Lake to Open Canyon and Coyote Lake. This means crossing deep snow until midseason. After the snow melts there are tricky talus fields to be negotiated. Check at Jenny Lake Ranger Station.

The Mt. Hunt Divide Trail now begins dropping toward the north fork of Granite Canyon. It becomes more difficult to follow as it gets lower. If you lose it, keep descending at the same grade to the bottom. The trail joins the Granite Canyon Trail 0.75 mi. above the Granite Canyon Patrol Cabin.

**Granite Canyon Parking Area (6,360 ft.)
to Open Canyon Trail (7,080 ft.)
and Phelps Lake (6,633 ft.)**

Mileage: 3.4 to Open Canyon Trail, 5.4 to Phelps Lake

Condition: Well maintained, easy hike.

Time: 1½ hrs. to Open Canyon Trail, 2½ hrs. to Phelps Lake.

(For a description of the trail from the Granite Canyon parking area to the Granite Canyon Ranger Station, see "Granite Canyon Parking Area to Marion Lake.")

This trail parallels the boundary of the JY Ranch, one of the largest inholdings remaining in Grand Teton National Park. The land on which this trail runs was donated to the park in 1962 by Laurence Rockefeller and was originally part of the JY. The Granite Canyon Patrol Cabin was one of the ranch cabins.

   From the junction east of the Granite Canyon Ranger Station the trail winds around the east slopes of Mt. Hunt and then climbs the Phelps Lake moraine. It is usually a little wet even though there is a bridge and a culvert. On top of the moraine the trail crosses the creek flowing out of Open Canyon (bridge). The Open Canyon Trail branches left (W) and goes up a ridge on the north shoulder of Open Canyon for 0.5 mi. where it joins the trail from White Grass Ranger Station. (For a description of the Open Canyon Trail from this point see "White Grass Ranger Station to Mt. Hunt Divide.")

   An eighth of a mile past the Open Canyon-Phelps Lake junction the trail reaches the top of the moraine directly above Phelps Lake. There is an unmarked junction here; keep left (N). The fork to the right (S) runs to the JY Ranch, which is private property.

   After paralleling the lake 0.25 mi. the trail reaches White Grass Ranger Station-Open Canyon Trail junction. If you wish to descend to the lake shore, go straight ahead 0.5 mi. on the White Grass Ranger Station Trail to the northwest shore.

> **Granite Canyon Parking Area (6,360 ft.)**
> **to Marion Lake (9,240 ft.)**
>
> Mileage: 8.8
>
> Condition: Well maintained, moderate hike.
>
> Time: 5 to 6 hrs.

This is the most recently constructed trail in Grand Teton National Park. It offers the opportunity to reach Marion Lake without having to cross the Mt. Hunt divide.

To reach the parking area, follow the highway north of Teton Village to the well-marked dirt road heading left (N). It is 2 mi. from the Teton Village turn-off to the Granite Canyon parking area.

From Moose, take the side road between the Visitor Center and the park entrance that goes south to Wilson (6 mi.). Motor homes and cars hauling large trailers should not use this route.

The trail heads due west from the parking area to the base of Apres Vous Peak (8,426 ft.). After crossing Granite Creek (bridge) it swings northwest, following the creek's west bank.

There is an unmarked trail junction 1 mi. from the parking area. The trail to the right (N) is the old Phelps Lake trail. It crosses the 2 channels of Granite Creek on makeshift bridges and in 0.5 mi. rejoins the new trail to Phelps Lake.

The old trail is the shorter one if you are going to Open Canyon Trail. If you hike to Phelps Lake you can use this trail on your return for a slight variation in route.

Take the left (W) fork following the south side of Granite Creek for the new trail. As it approaches the mouth of Granite Canyon, it is joined by the trail from Teton Village. (For a description see "Rendezvous Mountain to Teton Village.")

Where the trail once again crosses Granite Creek (bridge), the new trail to Open Canyon and Phelps Lake branches right (N). Keeping left (W), the Granite Canyon Trail passes the Granite Canyon Ranger Station and enters the canyon 1.6 mi. from the parking area. It climbs through a talus field onto the north slope of the canyon where it stays until near the head of the canyon.

This trail seems to offer more opportunity for seeing moose than any other. I always see 2 or more before reaching the forks.

The trail gradually climbs, sometimes staying high above the creek and sometimes winding through willows near the creek to the Granite Canyon Forks and the Granite Canyon Patrol Cabin. Here there is good water from springs and streams.

The Rendezvous Mountain Trail joins the Granite Canyon Trail from the left (S) 6.3 mi. from the parking area. Shortly after this junction the patrol cabin path (unmarked) leaves to the left. The trail gets a little steeper as it enter the north fork.

Campsite 31 is located 0.6 mi. past the Rendezvous Mountain Trail junction. The Mt. Hunt Divide-Open Canyon Trail junction is 0.1 mi. further. The sign posted here is helpful because the trail is hard to distinguish. (See "Mt. Hunt Divide to Granite Canyon Trail" for a description of this trail.)

The north fork widens here. The trail passes through

open meadows and then crosses the creek to the south side. There is no bridge, but adroit rock hopping will get you across with dry feet. This is easier in late season when there is less water.

The trail now begins to climb the south wall of the canyon to the Skyline or Teton Crest Trail junction, 8.2 mi. from the parking area. This section is usually very wet and slippery. Keeping right (N) at the junction, the trail to Marion Lake recrosses the north fork of Granite Creek (no bridge needed here) and climbs steeply toward the head of the canyon and Housetop Mountain.

When you reach the bench below the headwall, the trail turns sharply right (N) and continues to the top of the bench and then drops to Marion Lake. Campsite 32 is on the southeast shore of the lake.

Marion Lake (9,240 ft.)
to Moose Creek Divide (9,080 ft.) —
South Boundary of the Park

Mileage: 2.7

Condition: Well maintained, moderate hike.

Time: 2½ hrs.

(and the Game Creek spur)

(For a description of the trail from Marion Lake to the North Fork of Granite Creek, 0.6 mi., see "Granite Canyon Parking Area to Marion Lake.")

From the north fork junction the trail climbs steeply out of the canyon to a saddle west of Peak 9,814, which separates the north and middle forks of Granite Creek. On the top of this saddle, 1 mi. from Marion Lake, the Game Creek Trail branches right (W) to a divide on the park boundary above Game Creek (0.75 mi.). It is not advisable to take this trail which is seldom used, not maintained and snow covered till midseason. It is a steep pull to the divide, and it is almost as easy to pick your own route to the top. The trail provides access to the Game Creek Trail in Targhee National Forest beginning near Victor, Idaho. (For details see "Connecting Trails in Targhee National Forest.") For a short excursion, hike to the divide for the view. Tuck your pack under a rock. Unguarded packs have a way of disappearing.

After dropping from the saddle, the Skyline or Teton Crest Trail crosses the headwaters of the middle fork of Granite Creek. There are good campsites here.

The Middle Fork Cutoff Trail branches left (E) 2.1 mi. from Marion Lake and goes to the Rendezvous Mountain Trail. A large rock cairn and a new sign mark the spot. (For a description see "Rendezvous Mountain to Teton Village Parking Area.")

The trail is quite level along the east edge of the divide that separates Grand Teton National Park from Targhee National Forest. The south fork of Granite Canyon can be seen sloping off to the northeast.

As the trail nears the Moose Creek divide, it passes a small lake which is a good place to camp. There are several old horse trails south of the lake that climb the small ridge behind it. Stay on the right (SW) to the divide and the park boundary. (See "Coal Creek-Skyline Trail" and "Phillips Pass-Teton Crest Trail" in "Connecting Trails in Targhee National Forest.")

**Rendezvous Mountain (10,446 ft.)
to Teton Village Parking Area (6,311 ft.)**

Mileage: 12.3

Condition: New trail, well maintained, moderate hike.

Time: 4 to 6 hrs.

(and Middle Fork Cutoff and
route to Rendezvous Peak)

The Jackson Hole aerial tram enables those who might otherwise have trouble getting into the high country to see the splendor of the Tetons. A good way to take advantage of the tram is to hike down from the summit of Rendezvous Mountain back to the Teton Village parking area. This trail is also a shortcut to Marion Lake via the Middle Fork Cutoff.

From the tram station on top of the mountain, follow the trail down the south ridge to the saddle between Rendezvous Mountain and Peak 10,215. The trail drops into a large cirque, switching down to its bottom. It then climbs north to a viewpoint on the opposite ridge. From here the trail cuts back to the south, traversing the west slope of Peak 10,215.

As the trail drops into the south fork of Granite Canyon, it crosses several small streams. To the east of the last stream crossing, before the head of the canyon, is a steep talus slope.

If you wish to hike to the summit of Rendezvous Peak, leave the trail here and follow the base of this talus slope

until you enter a large cirque southeast of the south fork of
Granite Canyon. Keep heading up this cirque to the col
between Rendezvous Peak and Peak 10,706. This col is just
east of the head of the drainage and quite obvious. There
are some lovely meadows here. The 3 small streams flowing
through them form the headwaters of the south fork of
Granite Creek. Ascend the open slopes to the col. From
here the south summit (10,800 ft.) is an easy scramble.

If you wish to continue to the main summit 107 ft.
higher, traverse southwest 0.25 mi. along the summit ridge.
This requires climbing a short pitch just below the main
summit. The rock is rotten so be careful. The main summit
route is recommended for those with some mountaineering
experience. Check at Jenny Lake Ranger Station.

The trail to Teton Village continues around the head of
the south fork of Granite Canyon, past Campsite 33. As the
trail bends north 3.5 mi. from the tram station, the Middle
Fork Cutoff Trail branches left (W). There is a sign here,
otherwise it would be easy to miss. A small rock cairn also
marks the spot.

This 0.5 mi. trail connects the Skyline or Teton Crest
Trail to the Rendezvous Mountain Trail. It is slightly overgrown in spots, but there are rock cairns built along its
entire length. Marion Lake is just 2.1 mi. from the Middle
Fork-Teton Crest junction.

After passing the Middle Fork junction, the Teton Village Trail follows the top of a ridge which separates the
south and middle forks of Granite Canyon. It crosses several large open meadows before dropping into the north
fork. Here the descent is quicker, switching back twice before crossing the Middle Fork Creek (bridge) and then the
North Fork Creek (bridge) where you can see the Granite

Canyon Patrol Cabin to the northwest.

The trail goes several hundred yards north to the North Fork Trail, 5.2 mi. from the tram station. (For a description of the trail from here to the Granite Canyon Ranger Station, see "Granite Canyon Parking Area to Marion Lake.")

From the Ranger Station to Teton Village (2.4 mi.) the trail follows the base of Apres Vous Peak (8,426 ft.). There is a lot of horse traffic on this section of the trail. You leave the park 0.5 mi. before reaching Teton Village. There are several forks in the trail which lead back to the parking area.

RECOMMENDED LONGER HIKES

Skyline or Teton Crest Trail

This trail runs from the Moose Creek divide on the southern boundary of the park to the String Lake parking area via Marion Lake, Fox Creek Pass, Death Canyon Shelf, Mt. Meek Pass, Alaska Basin, Hurricane Pass, Lake Solitude, Paintbrush divide and Paintbrush Canyon.

Several connecting Teton National Forest trails offer different approaches to Moose Creek divide. I recommend the one from the foot of Teton Pass on the west side. A trail runs up Coal Creek to a saddle east of Taylor Mountain, down Mesquite Creek to Moose Creek and back up to the divide and the park boundary (7.5 mi.).

You can also take the Phillips Canyon Trail from north of Wilson to Phillips Pass, and then drop into Moose Creek on what the 1968 Rendezvous Peak quad calls the Teton Crest Trail. This trail joins the Moose Creek Trail just below the Moose Creek divide and the park boundary (9 mi.).

An easier route with less gain in altitude is from the Phillips Ridge road off the Teton Pass Highway. From this road a trail traverses into Phillips Canyon, joining the Phillips Canyon Trail 1.25 mi. below Phillips Pass. Total distance to Moose Creek divide and the park boundary is 7.7 mi.

It is also possible, though not recommended, to hike the Moose Creek Trail from its beginning near Victor, Idaho.

The total mileage for the old Skyline Trail from Coal Creek to String Lake parking area is 38.7 mi. The new Teton Crest Trail via Phillips Canyon is 40.2 mi. While this trip can be made in 2 days, I would suggest relaxing and taking 3 or 4 days to do it. (For a detailed description of the trail see the following: In "Trails in the Park"—"Marion Lake to Moose Creek Divide," "Fox Creek Pass to Marion Lake," "Basin Lakes to Fox Creek Pass," "Hurricane Pass to Basin Lakes," "Forks of Cascade Canyon to Hurricane Pass," "Jenny Lake to Lake Solitude," "Lake Solitude to Paintbrush Divide," "Paintbrush Divide to String Lake Parking Area"; in "Connecting Trails in Teton National Forest"—"Phillips Canyon Cutoff Trail"; in "Connecting Trails in Targhee National Forest"—"Coal Creek Campground to Moose Creek Divide," "Phillips Pass to Moose Creek Divide.")

Loop Hikes

The most popular loop has been from Jenny Lake to String Lake parking area via Lake Solitude and Paintbrush divide (19.5 mi.). This 2 day hike has been made more difficult by the fact that Lake Solitude and Holly Lake have been closed to camping. (For details see "Jenny Lake to Lake Solitude," "Lake Solitude to Paintbrush Divide" and "Paintbrush Divide to String Lake Parking Area.")

There are 2 possible loops from the White Grass Ranger Station. One is up Death Canyon to Fox Creek Pass, across the Death Canyon Shelf, over Mt. Meek Pass into Alaska Basin to the Static Peak divide and then back down into Death Canyon (24.9 mi.). Depending on how much time you wish to spend exploring Alaska Basin (no camping permits required), this trip can take 2 or 3 days. (For details see "White Grass Ranger Station to Fox Creek Pass," "Basin Lakes to Fox Creek Pass," "Upper Alaska Basin to Static Peak Divide" and "Static Peak Divide to Death Canyon Patrol Cabin.")

The second possibility is to hike up Death Canyon to Fox Creek Pass, past Spearhead Peak to Marion Lake, down Granite Canyon to Open Canyon Trail, over Mt. Hunt divide, down Open Canyon and back to the Death Canyon Trail at the inlet of Phelps Lake (24.7 mi.) This trip can be made in 2 or 3 days although it is more strenuous than the first. (For details see "White Grass Ranger Station to Fox Creek Pass," "Fox Creek Pass to Marion Lake," "Granite Canyon Parking Area to Marion Lake," "Mt. Hunt Divide to Granite Canyon Trail" and "White Grass Ranger Station to Mt. Hunt Divide.")

There are 2 possible loops from Granite Canyon parking area. The first goes up Granite Canyon to Open Canyon Trail junction, over Mt. Hunt divide, down Open Canyon and back to the point of origin via the Valley Trail (19.3 mi.). This loop can easily be made in 2 days, especially if you request an off-trail camping permit either for the Open Canyon Trail a mile or so below Mt. Hunt divide, or for Mt. Hunt divide on a bench overlooking Open Canyon. (For details see "Granite Canyon Parking Area to Marion Lake," "Mt. Hunt Divide to Granite Canyon Trail," "White Grass

Ranger Station to Mt. Hunt Divide" and "Granite Canyon Parking Area to Open Canyon Trail.")

The second and longer loop goes up Granite Canyon to Marion Lake, past Spearhead Peak to Fox Creek Pass, down Death Canyon to Phelps Lake and returns to Granite Canyon parking area via the Valley Trail (23.7 mi.). This loop can be hiked in 2 or 3 days. (For details see "Granite Canyon Parking Area to Marion Lake," "Fox Creek Pass to Marion Lake," "White Grass Ranger Station to Fox Creek Pass" and "Granite Canyon Parking Area to Open Canyon and Phelps Lake.")

The basic loop in the north end of the park is from the Berry Creek Ranger Station up Webb Canyon to the Moose Basin divide, down Owl Creek to lower Berry Creek, and back to the ranger station (20.2 mi.). This is a 2 day loop, but many variations are possible as all trails in the area return to the Berry Creek Ranger Station. (For details on the basic loop see "Berry Creek Ranger Station to Moose Basin Divide," "Moose Basin Divide to Junction of Owl Creek-Berry Creek Trails" and "Berry Creek Patrol Cabin to Berry Creek Ranger Station.")

Other loops are possible, especially from the Idaho side. Two of these are discussed in "Recommended Loop Trips in Targhee National Forest." With a little thought, you can plan a number of variations in the suggested trips. Be sure to check at Jenny Lake Ranger Station before leaving on off-trail hikes in Grand Teton National Park.

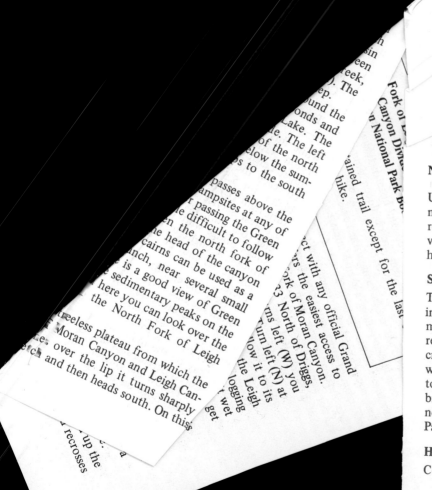

Connecting Trails in Targhee National Forest

NORTHERN SECTION

Unless you are a jeep-road or horse-packing buff, you will not find the next 4 trails in this section a practical way to reach the Tetons. Their drawbacks far outweigh their advantages. For this reason only a brief description is included here.

South Boone Creek to Survey Peak Area   7 mi.

The trail begins 28 mi. east of Ashton, Idaho, on the Hominy Peak spur of the old reclamation road. It is an old dirt mining road, suitable only for jeeps. This spur leaves the reclamation road north of Squirrel Meadows. The road crosses South Boone Creek 2 mi. from this junction. This is where the trail begins. It follows the north side of the creek to its head, where a fork to the Hominy Peak Trail (1.5 mi.) branches right (S). The main trail continues around the north side of Survey Peak to the Grand Teton National Park boundary.

Hominy Peak Spur and Trail to Jackass Pass   2 mi.

Continue 8 mi. from the South Boone Creek Trail on the

same jeep road to Hominy Peak (8,362 ft.), which
old Forest Service fire lookout. It is less than
Jackass Pass and the park boundary. I am told
experienced jeep driver can get through. A trai
right (S) to Conant Basin (1 mi.) and Conant Pa
0.5 mi. from the old lookout.

Dry Creek (McReynold Reservoir) to Conant

This trail begins at the end of a dirt road
community of Felt, Idaho, 5 mi. north of T
follows Dry Creek past McReynold Rese
drainage into Crater Creek, over another
Creek following the north fork to the
Creek flows into it. It then ascends
head which is just south of Conant Pa

South Fork of Bitch Creek
to Divide West of Moose Basin

(See "Dry Creek to Conant Pass
trail to the forks of Bitch Creek.

From the forks, the trail follow
into Hidden Corral Basin, from
swings north through the Moos
right (E) just before Nord Pass to th
Mountain. From here there is access to M
"Berry Creek Ranger Station to Moose Basin D.
"Trails in the Park.")

the tractor trail for 0.75 mi. until it reaches an unmarked
junction. The right (S) fork is the Andy Stone Trail, whic
continues up the main drainage southwest to Granite Ba
and the south fork of Leigh Creek. The left (E) fork, G
Mountain Trail, follows the north side of Tin Cup C
climbing the west slope of Green Mountain (9,614 ft
trail becomes a jeep trail at this point and is quite ste
At the bottom of the couloir the trail swings ar
east wall of Green Mountain. It passes 2 small
forks (unmarked) just before reaching Green divi
right (S) fork continues to Leigh Canyon divi
(E) fork passes the stepped lakes at the head
fork canyon, climbs the east wall, traverses b
mit of Green Lakes Mountain and then dr
fork of Badger Creek.

The trail to the Leigh Canyon divid
Green Mountain Lakes. There are go
the 4 lakes or 8 ponds in this area.
Mountain Lakes the trail becomes a litt
as it heads toward the divide betwe
Leigh Creek and Granite Basin. At t
the trail climbs out due east Rock
guide. This is a good sp for
ponds in an open mead . The
Mountain, which is ty cal of th
west slope of the Te ns. Fro
Green Mountain Lakes do
Creek.

The trail climbs to a h
divides to the south fork
yon are visible. As it
right for a very short s

plateau are some fine high country scenes: small waterfalls, streams, an abundance of wildflowers and the Grand Teton and Mt. Owen rising in the distance. To the west, the plateau slopes into Idaho and Pierre's Hole. There is good camping near several small ponds.

The trail continues south for 0.5 mi. and then turns right (W), dropping into Granite Basin. There is good camping at any of the 3 lakes below. It is possible to loop back to the north fork of Leigh Canyon (7.5 mi.) by taking the trail northwest from Granite Basin to the Andy Stone Trail (4 mi.). It is also possible to take the left (S) fork of this trail into the south fork of Leigh Creek. From here you can climb the plateau behind Fred's Mountain (Grand Targhee Ski Area), drop into the north fork of Teton Creek and follow it back to Teton Canyon Campground, 8 mi. from Granite Basin.

To reach the Leigh Canyon divide, leave Granite Basin Trail as it turns west. Follow a small drainage east toward the visible divide north of Little's Peak (10,712 ft.). It is an easy 0.5 mi. cross-country hike to the divide.

To descend the divide, swing northeast, avoiding the steep snow cornice, and follow the game trail into the canyon. It is not difficult if you are careful. There are good campsites at Mink Lake (permit required). (For a route to Cascade Canyon from Mink Lake see "Lake Solitude to Paintbrush Divide" in "Trails in Grand Teton National Park.") One can also bushwhack down Leigh Canyon to Leigh Lake (not recommended).

To reach the south fork of Moran Canyon, follow the Leigh Canyon divide north 1.25 mi. and drop off another, less steep divide into the canyon. It is also possible to continue northeast, past the game trail descending into Leigh

Canyon, to the divide below Maidenform Peak. This divide separates Leigh Canyon from the south fork of Moran Canyon. The descent of this divide is a bit steeper than the one 1.25 mi. north.

Teton Canyon Campground (6,955 ft.)
to Table Mountain (11,106 ft.)

Mileage: 5.5

Condition: Occasionally maintained, no bridges, trail ends on west ridge of mountain, route to summit a scramble, moderate hike except for summit.

Time: 4 hrs.

To reach Teton Canyon Campground follow the Grand Targhee Ski Area signs from Driggs, Idaho, through Alta, Wyoming, to the mouth of Teton Canyon (6 mi.). Take the right fork into the canyon; do not go to the ski area. Drive to the end of the road. The campground is 6.8 mi. from Alta.

From the campground cross the road to the well-marked trail up the north fork of Teton Creek. It climbs a short, steep ridge, passing a waterfall to the relatively flat lower canyon. There are good campsites here. Past the campground 1.4 mi., an unmarked trail branches sharply left (NW). This trail climbs out of the north fork of Teton Creek and drops into the south fork of Leigh Creek, eventually connecting with the north fork of Leigh Creek in Granite Basin. (See "North Fork of Leigh Creek to Leigh Canyon Divide" for details.)

The Table Mountain Trail continues up the north side of the creek, crossing it as the canyon swings southeast. Two logs are lashed together to form a bridge. The trail becomes steep as it climbs through some small alpine meadows. The flowers are spectacular here in July and August.

After reaching a small bench the trail crosses the creek again. Go downstream and cross on the beaver dam. You must cross it again where the creek swings east. This crossing can be made by hopping rocks, except in early season.

As the trail enters the large cirque at the head of the canyon the summit of Table Mountain can be seen to the southeast. After crossing a small creek (good log here) the trail turns west and begins to climb the west headwall. **WARNING**: The trail is snow covered in early season. Bring an ice axe. Switch up the headwall to the top (9,945 ft.). The trail then goes to the summit block of Table Mountain. It peters out in the talus 0.5 mi. before the summit block is reached.

To ascend to the summit, scramble up the obvious routes used by others. There is a good view of the south fork of Cascade Canyon and the Grand Teton from an overlook to the east of the summit block. Follow the path around the summit on the south side to reach the 2 viewpoints. The one farther east has the better view. It is 2,000 ft. straight down to Cascade Canyon, making this one of the most spectacular viewpoints in the Tetons. In 1872 William Jackson took the first photographs of the Tetons from this area.

> **Table Mountain (11,106 ft.)**
> **to Hurricane Pass (10,372 ft.)**
> Mileage: 1.5
> Condition: No trail, difficult hike.
> Time: 1 hr.

This traverse can be used by those continuing into Grand
Teton National Park or returning via Alaska Basin to the
Teton Canyon Campground. It is recommended for the ex-
perienced hiker only.

From south of the summit block, follow the ridge down
to the col between Table Mountain and Peak 10,635. Be
careful descending this steep ridge. There is a good campsite
just east of the col (10,121 ft.) overlooking Cascade Canyon.

Contour around Peak 10,635 to the west, losing as little
elevation as possible. Head for the south ridge of the peak.
A short scramble takes you to its top. The rock is limestone
and sloughs off easily. Once on the south ridge, it is a short
descent to Hurricane Pass and the trail to Alaska Basin.

You can descend Roaring Creek from either the col
south of Table Mountain or from Hurricane Pass, but this
route is not recommended because the scramble is steep
near the bottom. You can also descend into Cascade Canyon from the col south of Table Mountain, but the trail
down from Hurricane Pass is easier.

> **Teton Canyon Campground (6,955 ft.)**
> **to Basin Lakes (9,550 ft.)**
>
> Mileage: 7.0
>
> Condition: Well maintained, moderate hike.
>
> Time: 5 to 6 hrs.

This trail offers the best approach to the Tetons from the west side. It is also closed to motorized vehicles and no sheep grazing permits have been issued here. (For details on the route to the Teton Canyon Campground see "Teton Canyon Campground to Table Mountain.")

From the campground, follow the jeep track up the canyon to the trail head. The trail is fairly level for 2.5 mi. Roaring Creek flows down from the east wall into Teton Creek 0.25 mi. past the first creek crossing (bridge). In 2.8 mi. the Teton Canyon Shelf Trail via the Devil's Stairs branches right (S). (See "Teton Canyon Shelf to Teton Canyon Campground" for a description.)

Past this junction the Alaska Basin Trail begins to climb more steeply, ascending a glacial bench after several switchbacks. There are good campsites on the bench. In 0.5 mi. it switches up another bench, crossing Teton Creek (bridge) to the north side. As it reaches the upper canyon it passes a Forest Service campsite with a table, fire grill and outhouse. From here the trail switches up the north wall and onto another bench, the last before reaching Alaska Basin.

Buck Mountain is visible to the east as you pass many small streams. There are lots of wildflowers in the open meadows. One switchback takes the trail to the headwall of the last bench. The wall is ascended via a series of switchbacks on the north side of a spring-fed stream.

Once over the lip, the trail joins the Skyline or Teton Crest Trail to the Basin Lakes, 0.25 mi. away. This trail is visible to the north as it switches down into the basin from Sunset Lake.

Teton Canyon Shelf (9,740 ft.)
to Teton Canyon Campground (6,955 ft.)

Mileage: 6.6

Condition: Occasionally maintained, Devil's Stairs a bit rough, easy hike.

Time: 4 hrs.

This trail can be used as a loop return to the Teton Canyon Campground from the Basin Lakes.

From its junction with the Teton Crest Trail 2 mi. south of Basin Lakes, the Teton Canyon Shelf Trail (right fork) follows the shelf as it swings west above Teton Canyon. The shelf offers many fine campsites because it is relatively flat. There is a good view across Alaska Basin to Battleship Mountain.

At 3.5 mi. from its junction with the Teton Crest trail you will come to the Devil's Stairs. These aptly named switchbacks take the trail down from the Teton Canyon Shelf to Teton Creek via a notch caused by water running down the limestone wall. I do not recommend that you go up the Devil's Stairs, especially with a heavy pack.

(For a description of the section from the junction with the Teton Canyon Trail to the campground, see "Teton Canyon Campground to the Basin Lakes.")

Darby Canyon Parking Area (7,069 ft.)
to Fox Creek Pass (9,600 ft.)

Mileage: 5.75

Condition: Well maintained to Wind Cave, then becomes difficult.

Time: 5 hrs.

This is a beautiful hike. The only drawback is the poor
condition of the higher section of the trail.

To reach the Darby Canyon parking area, turn east off
Idaho 33, 5 mi. north of Victor, Idaho, onto the Darby
Canyon Road. Follow this road 7.7 mi. to its end and park.

Cross Darby Creek (bridge) to the well-worn trail heading east. In the lower section there is some confusion because a new trail has been cleared and the old one is still
used by horse parties. Both trails end at the same spot. The
newer one is less steep and crosses the old one a number of
times. Follow the more gradually climbing trail.

The trail crosses the south fork of Darby Creek. In early
season you will have to wade it. Later, rock hopping will
get you across. The trail then turns up the south fork of the
canyon and climbs to a bench where limestone walls cross
the canyon. Above them on the bench, the trail follows the
left (E) bank of the creek. The Wind Cave can be seen
across the canyon above a waterfall.

The trail turns sharply right (W), crosses the south fork
of the creek and heads directly for the Wind Cave. Just
before reaching the cave, the trail to upper Darby Canyon is
supposed to fork left (S) after crossing a small stream. The
trail is not visible at this point, nor is it marked.

The Wind Cave is very interesting. Leave your pack at the bottom and follow the path up to a stone monument. From here it is a scramble to the mouth of the cave. The best way to enter the cave is by crossing the stream which flows out of it to the north side and climbing a series of ledges. Bring a flashlight if you want to explore much farther. It is 2 mi. from the parking area to the cave.

At the point of the supposed trail junction, head up the small stream (in late season it is dry) 0.25 mi., then head southeast across the small ridge separating this stream from the South Fork Creek. Look for rock cairns. The Wind Cave Trail turns due east after 0.7 mi. and crosses the South Fork Creek. Look up and down the creek to find the trail. It is marked by rock cairns.

Again the trail climbs the east slope to avoid the limestone walls. Once above them it swings around the west face of Fossil Mountain to a saddle west of the summit. Since you are above the timberline the route to this saddle is obvious even if you cannot find the trail. Watch for mountain sheep near the saddle.

A descent from the saddle into Fox Creek can be very tricky in early season because there is a large snow cornice blocking the route. Even in late season there is not much more than a goat path down. Watch for falling rock. A staff would be a good idea here, especially if you are carrying a heavy pack. An ice axe is necessary in early season.

After negotiating this stretch, the trail gets easier. To avoid losing elevation, bear left at the bottom of the saddle on an unmarked path towards Fox Creek Pass. There are many hunting trails and camps in the area. This path takes you to a hunting camp on the north branch of Fox Creek.

Cross the creek to Fox Creek Trail and follow it up to Fox Creek Pass, staying on the north side all the way. This trail is frequently used and easy to find.

SOUTHERN SECTION

The following 3 trails are not recommended for reasons described below.

Fox Creek to Fox Creek Pass   7.1 mi.

Follow Idaho 33 north from Victor, Idaho, for 3 mi. to a gravel road. Turn right (E) at the sign and follow this road 4 mi. to its end. The trail begins at a Forest Service sign and passes through U and I Sugar Company's calcium phosphate quarry which is at the mouth of Fox Creek Canyon. This is private property on which blasting frequently occurs. In addition, many unbridged creek crossings and confusing horse trails make this a trail to be avoided.

Game Creek to Game Creek Divide   9 mi.

This trail begins on private property 3 mi. southeast of Victor, Idaho, on the old Teton Pass Road. Go south on the road across Game Creek and take the second road to the left (E) past the creek. Follow this dirt road past a house and into the canyon. Park at the unbridged creek crossing. The Forest Service does not maintain this trail. There are no signs, numerous unbridged creek crossings, and you are trespassing in reaching the trail head. The trail is used mostly by hunters and sheepherders and is in poor condition on the Grand Teton National Park side.

Moose Creek to Moose Creek Divide   7 mi.

The trail begins 3.3 mi. from the Teton Pass Highway at the
end of a poorly maintained dirt road. The junction is 3.5
mi. southeast of Victor, Idaho. It is often possible to get a
car to within 0.5 mi. of the road's end. Keep right (S) at the
forks. The left (N) fork goes to a picnic spot near the creek
across from Plummer Canyon. The right fork passes Nord-
wall Canyon and the trail to Taylor Basin and Taylor Mountain and then continues into the canyon. Park at Bear Canyon and walk to the trail head.

It does not make much sense to hike to Moose Creek
divide this way. It is used mostly by horse parties. Ignore
Forest Service distances on the sign at the road junction. It
is 3.75 mi. of wet creek bottom to Moose Meadows, with 2
unbridged creek crossings.

To reach Moose Creek divide, use either the Skyline
Trail from Coal Creek or the Teton Crest Trail from Phillips
Pass.

**Coal Creek Campground (7,280 ft.)
to Moose Creek Divide (9,080 ft.)—
Grand Teton National Park Boundary**

Mileage: 7.5

Condition: Occasionally maintained, no bridges, mod-
       erate hike.

Time: 5 to 6 hrs.

At the foot of Teton Pass on the west side is an undeveloped Forest Service campground north of the highway. It
contains a few tables, an outhouse, and creek water for

drinking. A Forest Service sign indicates the Skyline Trail. I recommend this approach to the Tetons as one of the best. Hiking from here to the String Lake parking area 38.7 mi. via the Skyline or Teton Crest Trail is a good way to explore the range. The Coal Creek section of the trail is not heavily used either by hikers or horse parties.

From the campground, follow the jeep trail north to where several trees lashed together form a bridge. Cross here and go up the creek. The trail crosses the creek 3 more times. The Forest Service usually cuts down a tree to bridge these spots; occasionally rock hopping or wading will be the only way to get across. After passing the forks, the trail climbs more steeply, switching back from an open meadow into a grove of aspen.

Below the east slope of Taylor Mountain are the Coal Creek Meadows, as beautiful as any alpine meadows you are likely to find. At the end of these meadows, as the trail starts up to a saddle, a branch trail forks left (W) and heads up the slopes of the north summit of Taylor Mountain (10,068 ft.), passing just south of the summit and dropping into Taylor Basin and then Moose Creek. If you have time, leave your pack near the junction and hike to the south summit of Taylor Mountain for a good view. If you are camping in the Coal Creek meadows a side trip to Taylor Basin is worthwhile.

The Skyline Trail continues north to the saddle (9,197 ft.) from where you can follow the right (E) ridge into upper Phillips Canyon on a game trail.

After dropping from the saddle, the trail passes through high meadows, now following the Mesquite Creek drainage. An unmarked trail branches right (E) to Phillips Pass 1 mi. below the saddle. It is obscured by high grass. The trail branches in an open area west of Phillips Pass.

The Skyline Trail becomes a bit difficult to follow as it drops sharply into Moose Creek. Stay on the west side of Mesquite Creek. At Moose Meadows the trail crosses Moose Creek to join the Moose Creek Trail, 3.5 mi. from Coal Creek Campground. Here you must wade the creek. There are several campsites in Moose Meadows near the trail junction.

Take the right (E) fork at the Moose Creek Trail junction passing on the west side of the meadow. At the north end you will have to wade the creek again.

Now the trail begins to climb the west slope of Rendezvous Peak. Near the head of the canyon it switches back once and crosses a stream above the main creek. Here an unmarked trail branches right (W) to Moose Lake (1.5 mi.) where there is a good campsite. If you do not see the branch trail at this point, continue to the main creek, cross it and follow the west bank until the trail becomes visible. It then follows Moose Creek to just below Moose Lake where it swings south and climbs into the cirque in which the lake is situated.

The Skyline Trail climbs toward the Moose Creek divide to the right (E). Past the Moose Lake Trail junction 0.25 mi., the Teton Crest Trail from Phillips Pass joins the Skyline Trail from the right (S). A series of switchbacks brings the trail to the top of the divide and the Grand Teton National Park boundary.

Phillips Pass (8,932 ft.)
to Moose Creek Divide (9,080 ft.)—
Grand Teton National Park Boundary
Mileage: 3.75
Condition: Seldom maintained, moderate hike.
Time: 2 hrs.

(See "Phillips Canyon Parking Area to Phillips Pass" in "Connecting Trails in Teton National Forest" for a description of the trail to this point.)

From the top of Phillips Pass the trail climbs the southwest slope of the south ridge of Rendezvous Peak, reaching an elevation of 9,760 ft. near the top. There is a good view down Moose Creek into Idaho. The trail is fairly easy to follow except in early season when snow covered. Deer are often seen grazing on these slopes.

The trail angles down the south summit into Moose Creek. It stays above the creek, contouring across the east slope of the canyon until it joins the Moose Creek Trail 3.5 mi. from Phillips Pass. From this junction the trail switchbacks up to the Moose Creek divide.

RECOMMENDED LOOP HIKES

Teton Canyon is the best spot to explore the western slope of the Tetons. Two loops are possible from the Teton Canyon Campground. The first follows the North Fork Trail to

Table Mountain, traverses to Hurricane Pass, follows the Teton Crest Trail to the Basin Lakes and comes down the south fork of Teton Canyon to the campground (17 mi.). This is a pleasant 2 day trip offering a wide variety of terrain, but should be attempted by experienced hikers only. (See "Teton Canyon Campground to Table Mountain," "Table Mountain to Hurricane Pass," "Hurricane Pass to Basin Lakes" in "Trails in Grand Teton National Park," and "Teton Canyon Campground to Basin Lakes" for details.)

The second loop is a hike up the south fork of Teton Creek to the Basin Lakes. Go up the Sheep Steps to Teton Canyon Shelf, follow the shelf to Devil's Stairs, drop back into the south fork of Teton Creek and return to the campground (15.6 mi.). This is an easier 2 day hike than the first and can be made by anyone. (See "Teton Canyon Campground to Basin Lakes," "Basin Lakes to Fox Creek Pass" in "Trails in Grand Teton National Park," and "Teton Canyon Shelf to Teton Canyon Campground" for details.)

There are other loop trips in Targhee National Forest, including the north fork of Leigh Creek to Granite Basin. Use your imagination in planning one.

Connecting Trails
in Teton National Forest

**Phillips Canyon Parking Area (6,320 ft.)
to Phillips Pass (8,932 ft.)**

Mileage: 5.0

Condition: Occasionally maintained, no bridges, moderate hike.

Time: 4 hrs.

To reach the parking area, take the paved road going north from Wilson, Wyoming. The pavement runs out in 1.25 mi. Follow this dead-end road for 3 mi. to the Forest Service sign and gate on the left (W) side of the road and park.

The first part of the trail follows a power line access road which is closed to public cars or trucks. This road has been washed out at the first creek crossing. A narrow log spans the creek, but to reach it is a bit tricky. In 0.4 mi. the trail leaves the access road, branching right (N) at the sign. It continues up the canyon following the north side of the creek, climbing a small ridge and then dropping to the creek and crossing it. There is no bridge here, but you can jump across except in early season. After 0.25 mi. the trail crosses the creek to the north side again. There is no bridge, but it is an easy jump.

The trail climbs gently through a large open area until it fords the north fork of Phillips Creek. It then climbs the ridge separating the north and middle forks. Swinging into the north fork, it goes to the junction of the Phillips Canyon Cutoff Trail, 1.25 mi. below Phillips Pass.

The middle canyon opens up and there are many good campsites in the area. Several paths branch left to those more frequently used. As the trail climbs the north slope of the canyon, keep to the right (N) at all forks. Head for the pass northwest of the canyon's head. Look for tall poles marking the trail. The trail follows a small drainage to a plateau below the pass. Here another trail branches left (SW) to a good campsite and the upper canyon.

The Phillips Pass Trail follows the same drainage to the pass. From here you can see Moose Creek. The Teton Crest Trail turns sharply right (E) on top of the pass and heads up the shoulder of the south ridge of Rendezvous Peak. (See "Phillips Pass to Moose Creek Divide-Teton Crest Trail" in "Connecting Trails in Targhee National Forest" for a description.)

**Phillips Canyon Cutoff Trail (7,920 ft.)
to Phillips Pass Trail (8,932 ft.)**

Mileage: 3.5

Condition: Well maintained, moderate hike.

Time: 2 hrs.

This trail saves some time and effort in reaching Phillips Pass and the Teton Crest Trail. To reach the trail parking area, take Wyoming 22 up Teton Pass, about half way to where the highway turns north. A dirt road branches right (N) 0.3 mi. farther. This is the Phillips Ridge Road, usually passable by car. Follow this road 0.5 mi. to the Forest Service sign on the left (N) side and park. The trail climbs a small knoll and parallels the road 0.5 mi. It then angles up the east slope of Mt. Glory. After reaching a bench it swings north through wet meadows.

Past the parking area 0.75 mi., an unmarked trail branches left (W) to Ski Lake (1 mi.). The cutoff continues toward Phillips Canyon 1 mi. past the Ski Lake Trail junction. It now drops into the canyon, crossing a slide area under the northernmost summit of Mt. Glory. The wildflowers here are plentiful. The trail drops to the creek 2.5 mi. from the parking area and crosses it. Rock hopping will get you across except in early season. The Phillips Canyon Trail junction is just across the creek. Take the left (W) fork to the pass. (For a description of the trail from this junction to Phillips Pass see "Phillips Canyon Parking Area to Phillips Pass.")

Appendices

AT HOME RECIPES

Granola

8 c. rolled oats
2 c. raw wheat germ
1 c. sesame seeds
1 c. unsweetened flaked coconut
2 c. raisins or other dried fruit
2 c. nuts (walnuts, cashews, etc.)
1 c. honey
¼ c. molasses
¼ c. cooking oil
2 tbs. soy sauce
2 tbs. vanilla

In a large bowl mix together rolled oats, wheat germ, sesame seeds and coconut. Heat honey, molasses, oil, soy sauce and vanilla until it pours easily. Pour honey mixture over oat mixture, stirring well to coat each particle. Spread on greased baking sheets and toast in a slow (300°) oven 15-25 minutes until golden brown, stirring occasionally. Cool, add raisins and nuts, and store tightly covered at room temperature.

Other grains and seeds may be added to the basic recipe.

Med Bennett's High Altitude Gorp

Combine and store in plastic bags or covered jars:
1 lb. roasted soybeans
½ lb. roasted sunflower seeds (salted)
¼ lb. roasted pumpkin seeds
¼ lb. macro flaked wheat
½ lb. pecans or other nuts

Jerky in the Oven

3 lbs. lean meat (beef, moose, etc.)
½ tsp. Liquid Smoke in 2 tbs. water
Salt and pepper to taste

Slice meat ¼ in. thick and remove all fat. Lay in a single layer on counter top and brush each piece with Liquid Smoke mixture. Salt generously, pepper as desired. Layer meat strips in large bowl or crock; put plate and a weight on top. Let stand at least 6 hrs. Remove meat from bowl and pat dry with paper towels. Stretch meat strips across oven racks, being careful not to overlap. Leave room for air to circulate; don't cover entire rack. Set oven as low as possible (150°) and let meat dry 11 hrs. Cool and store in air-tight container.

CAMPGROUNDS AND CAMPSITES IN
GRAND TETON NATIONAL PARK
(south to north)

Reservations are now required for Jenny Lake, Signal Mountain and Colter Bay campgrounds. They can be made anywhere in the country through American Express (service charge $1.50), or you can write directly to the park. The other campgrounds are available on a first-come, first-served basis.

CAMPGROUNDS: (Usually full by early evening.)

Gros Ventre—Least desirable, easiest to get into. Located on the road to Kelly. Turn east off U.S. 89-187 6 mi. north of Jackson and go 4.5 mi. to the campground on the south side of the road; located on the bank of the Gros Ventre River.

Jenny Lake—Most desirable, hardest to get into. No trailers or campers allowed, tents only. Located on the east shore of Jenny Lake.

Signal Mountain—Recently enlarged. Located on the east shore of Jackson Lake. Easy to get to from Jenny Lake or Moran Junction.

Colter Bay—Largest, with the most facilities, including nearby showers, laundry, restaurant, tap room, grocery store, etc. Located on the east shore of Jackson Lake 5 mi. north of Jackson Lake Lodge.

Lizard Creek—Located on Fonda Point on the east shore of Jackson Lake near the north boundary of the park. A little too far from the center of things, but provides easy access by boat to Webb Creek, Owl Creek and Berry Creek 0.5 mi. across the lake.

CAMPSITES:

As of the summer of 1973, camping was permitted in most parts of the park. There are no designated campsites other than 1-17, but the areas in which one may camp vary only slightly from the list below. It is now possible to make reservations for 30% of the backcountry campsites. Permits must be picked up by noon on the day of the trip. The rest are available on a first-come, first-served basis. There is a 3 day limit to camping in any 1 spot in the backcountry.

Campsite	No. of Campsites	Location
1. Berry Creek	3	At Hechtman Creek
1A. Upper Berry Creek	3	In upper end of Berry Creek Meadows
2. Mouth of Berry Creek	1	On Jackson Lake south of Berry Creek
3. Warm Springs	3	South of Warm Springs, on Jackson Lake
4. Moran Bay	2	At the west end of Moran Bay south of the inlet
5. Bearpaw Bay	2	At the south end of Bearpaw Bay near the creek
5A. Little Grassy Island	1	On Little Grassy Island
6. Spalding Bay	3	On the west shore of Spalding Bay

Campsite	No. of Campsites	Location
6A. Deadman Point	2	On the island near Deadman Point
7. South Landing	3	On the southeast shore of South Landing
8. Hermitage Point	2	On the southeast shore of Hermitage Point
9. Elk Island	3	On the southeast shore of Elk Island
10. Little Mackinaw Bay	2	On the north shore of Little Mackinaw Bay
11. Two Ocean Lake	4	Near the outlet at the end of the road
12. Leigh Lake	3	On the east shore
13. Leigh Lake	1	On the west shore of the south bay
14. Leigh Lake	2	On the west side near the inlet from Leigh Canyon
15. Holly Lake	5	On the south and east sides of the lake, horse parties 0.25 mi. below lake.
17. Cascade Canyon	3	In the North Fork, 4.5 mi. from west Jenny Lake dock
18. Cascade Canyon	5	3.5 mi. from west Jenny Lake dock, 0.5 mi. below Forks Junction
19. Cascade Canyon	3	5.5 mi. from west Jenny Lake dock in the South Fork

Campsite	No. of Camp-sites	Location
19A. Cascade Canyon-South Fork Horse Camp	2	6.5 mi. from west Jenny Lake dock in the South Fork
20. Cascade Canyon	5	8 mi. from west Jenny Lake dock in the South Fork
21. Amphitheater Lake	5	On the north side of Amphitheater Lake, issued only at Jenny Lake Ranger Station
22. Surprise Lake	3	On the north side of Surprise Lake
26. Death Canyon	3	4 mi. from White Grass Ranger Station
27. Death Canyon	3	6.5 mi. from White Grass Ranger Station
28. Phelps Lake	3	On the northeast side of Phelps Lake
29. Open Canyon	1	5.5 mi. from White Grass Ranger Station
30. Granite Canyon	3	4.5 mi. from Granite Canyon parking area
31. Granite Canyon	3	6.5 mi. from Granite Canyon parking area
32. Marion Lake	3	On east side of Marion Lake
33. Granite Canyon	3	8 mi. from Granite Canyon parking area in the South Fork

Where numbers are missing, campsites have been phased out.

CAMPGROUNDS IN
TARGHEE NATIONAL FOREST

There are 6 campgrounds in the Snake River Canyon between Alpine Junction and Hoback Junction at the confluence of the Snake and Hoback rivers on U.S. 89.

There are 2 campgrounds between Victor, Idaho and Teton Pass on Idaho 33-Wyoming 22. Coal Creek Campground (undeveloped) provides access to the Skyline Trail. It is located at the foot of Teton Pass on the Idaho side, and has a few tables, an outhouse, and creek water for drinking.

The only developed Forest Service campground that provides easy access to the Tetons is on the Idaho side of the mountains in Teton Canyon. From Driggs, Idaho, take the gravel road to Alta, Wyoming, then east up Teton Canyon 7 mi. to Teton Canyon Campground.

CAMPGROUNDS IN
TETON NATIONAL FOREST

Atherton Creek—Located on Lower Slide Lake. Take the paved road up the Gros Ventre River 1 mi. north of Kelly. Pavement ends at this campground.

Curtis Canyon—Great view of the Tetons. Easy access to Jackson 7 mi. away. Follow the road through the National Elk Refuge northeast of Jackson to the well-marked Curtis Canyon turn-off. Located on a bench overlooking the valley.

Crystal Creek—Located 0.25 mi. past Red Hills Campground on the left.

Hatchet—Located just past (E) the Hatchet Motel at the foot of Togwotee Pass on U.S. 89.

Lava Creek—Very small. Located 3 mi. east of Moran Junction on Highway 89 just outside the Grand Teton National Park boundary.

Red Hills—Located on the Gros Ventre River 6 mi. past Atherton Creek Campground. Road is very slippery when wet.

There are 2 campgrounds in Hoback Canyon and 1 campground near Granite Hot Springs in Granite Canyon.

FISHING INFORMATION AND REGULATIONS IN GRAND TETON NATIONAL PARK

Fishing is permitted in Grand Teton National Park in conformance with laws and regulations of the State of Wyoming, subject to regulations of National Park Service.

Licenses: A Wyoming State fishing license is required for:
1. **Resident Persons**—14 years of age or over. **Cost:** $3
2. **Non-resident Persons**—regardless of age, unless under 14 years of age *and* in the company of a person in possession of a valid fishing license. Creel limit of such person under 14 years of age shall be applied to and limited by the fishing license held by the person in his company. **Cost:** Annual: $12. 5 day: $4

Fishing Hours: 4:00 A.M. to 10:00 P.M. Mountain Standard or Daylight Time.

Creel Limit: 8 lbs. and 1 fish not to exceed 6 trout per day or in possession.

Exceptions: 1. *Whitefish* creel limit 25 per day, regardless of weight, with a possession limit of 3 days' catch. 2. *Brook trout:* 8 lbs. and 1 fish not to exceed 10 fish per day or in possession. (A mixed catch of brook trout and other trout will not exceed 8 lbs. and 1 fish or contain more than 6 trout other than brook.

Seasons:
Snake River: April 1-October 31; whitefish *only*; open all year.

Cottonwood Creek: July 1-October 31.

All other streams, lakes and beaver ponds (including tributary streams and springs of the Snake River): May 30-October 31.

Jackson Lake: January 1-September 30 and November 1-December 31.

Jenny and Leigh lakes: open all year.

Legal Fishing Tackle: One rod or pole with no more than 3 hooks attached and the fisherman in attendance is the only lawful means of taking fish.

Closed Waters: The following waters are closed to fishing at all times: The Snake River for a distance of 150 ft. below Jackson Lake Dam; Cottonwood Creek from the outlet of Jenny Lake to the Saddle Horse Concession bridge; Swan Lake; Christian and Sawmill ponds and Hedrick's Pond.

Bridges and Docks: Fishing from any bridge or dock is prohibited.

Bait: The use or possession of fish eggs or fish for bait is prohibited in all park waters, *except* that it is permissible to use *dead* nongame fish along the shore or on Jackson Lake at any time, and along the shores or on Leigh and Jenny lakes from December 1-April 30. Other types of live bait (worms, grasshoppers, etc.) are permitted, but digging for or collecting bait (including nongame species) is prohibited within the park.

Field Notes